# MURDER & SCANDAL in PROHIBITION PORTLAND

# MURDER & SCANDAL in PROHIBITION PORTLAND

## SEX, VICE & MISDEEDS in MAYOR BAKER'S REIGN

JD CHANDLER AND
THERESA GRIFFIN KENNEDY

THE History PRESS

Published by The History Press
Charleston, SC
www.historypress.net



First published 2016

Manufactured in the United States

ISBN 978.1.46711.953.5

Library of Congress Control Number: 2015956821

*Stop bragging. All cities are like that.*
*—Lincoln Steffens*

# CONTENTS

# ACKNOWLEDGEMENTS

First and foremost, I must thank Mr. JD Chandler, writer and crime historian extraordinaire, for inviting me to be a part of this project. JD's faith in my writing skills and research abilities continue to move me to give thanks that there are writers as skilled and prolific as he is, who promote and support the work of other writers who are less known. That level of generosity is rare in the world of writing and publishing today and sorely needed. I must also thank those people who helped in my research, such as Brian Johnson and Mary Hansen of the Portland Archives and Records Center, who made those thrilling "aha!" moments possible when searching through countless, dusty police personnel files from seventy and eighty years ago. I would like to thank Scott Daniels of the Oregon Historical Society for his generous assistance in helping me with the selection and purchase of images for the book, which proved to be a challenging endeavor. Lastly, I must thank my husband, Don DuPay, for his unfailing support and encouragement and for his expert speculative opinions regarding police politics and police culture of long ago. I would like to thank others for their friendship and support as well, including J.B. Fisher, Phil Stanford and all the supporting staff at The History Press who make books like this possible. Where there is the time and the resources, there will always be people like JD and myself, trying to apprehend those forgotten scenarios and make them approachable for all to enjoy and learn from in the decades to come.

–Theresa Griffin Kennedy

# ACKNOWLEDGEMENTS

There are two questions people ask me on a regular basis—well, actually three, but I won't talk about my clothing choices right now: why do you focus on such dark subjects? Doesn't your work make you cynical? Everybody asks these things, and I have been struggling for a good answer that I can give when it comes up. I haven't got it yet, but I know two things: life is dark whether I make that choice or not, and in the words of Lily Tomlin, "No matter how cynical I get, I just can't keep up." I love learning about the criminal activities of our grandparents and the worst things that people can do to each other. Deep inside me is an eight-year-old boy who loves gore and scary stuff, delights in the humor of Alfred Hitchcock and can't get enough of the chills. And I like history, too. Thanks to Theresa Griffin Kennedy for encouraging me in my madness and Dawn O'Neill for aiding and abetting my activities. All the usual suspects (and a few new ones): Barney Blalock, Steve Chandler, Don Dupay, Carie Eisler, J.B. Fisher, Gary Flynn, Julie Generic, Ken Goldstein, Mary Hammer, Jim Huff, Michael Munk, Shirley Obitz, Zach Ollila, Leslie Sands, Austin Schultz, Brittany Sharp, Phil Stanford, Nancy Stewart, Jake Warren, Stephen Weinstein, Fred Stewart (super sponsor) and all the patrons and "first lookers" at www.patreon.com/jdchandler. Support your local historian.

Thanks for reading.

–JD Chandler

INTRODUCTION

# THE LIQUOR QUESTION

[Prohibition] *can't stop what it's meant to stop.*
*We like it.*
*It's left a trail of graft and slime*
*It's filled our land with vice and crime.*
*It don't prohibit worth a dime,*
*Nevertheless, we're for it.*
*—Franklin P. Adams*

The first decade of the twentieth century was an exciting time in Portland. The Progressive movement, under the leadership of William U'Ren and others, expanded democracy through its innovative Oregon System, which included the direct election of senators, citizen initiative, referendum and recall elections, as well as open primaries. In 1912, when women finally achieved the vote in Oregon, it seemed as if anything was possible with more opportunities and a surging hope for women's concerns. In 1913, when the women working at the Oregon Packing Company cannery on Southeast Morrison Street walked out on strike, the Industrial Workers of the World (IWW) supported them and began a campaign to win public support for their cause and create a general strike. The IWW, members of which were known as Wobblies, was a radical labor organization that avoided politics and embraced workplace action instead. Wobblies organized the most exploited of the poor, female and child workers, transient laborers and the unemployed in order to build power. They organized across racial lines and

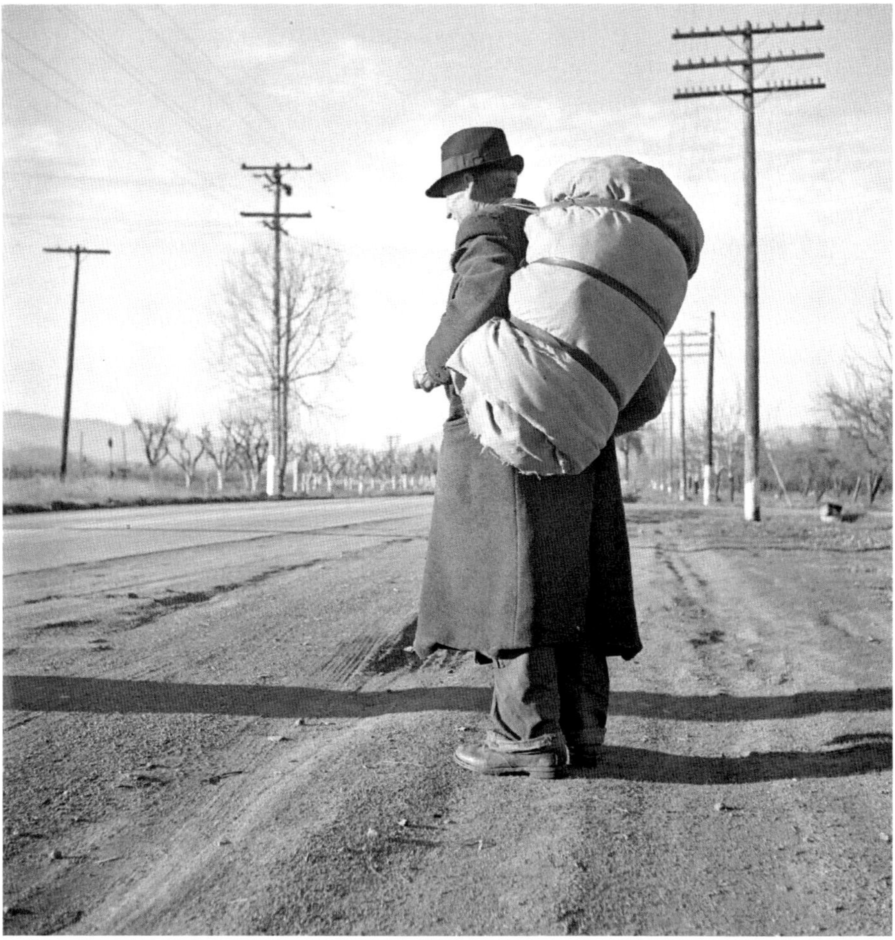

Bindle stiffs, who walked or "rode the rails" from job to job carrying their belongings in bindles, made up the majority of membership in the Industrial Workers of the World (IWW). Photograph by Dorothea Lang. *U.S. Library of Congress.*

emphasized class consciousness and direct action through work slowdowns and stoppages. Their goal was to create a general strike in which all of the city's workers would rise up to seize the means of production and end the capitalist system, which they called "wage slavery," impacting the most vulnerable.

Wobblies used cultural resistance as the strategy of their organizing, using songs, jokes and cartoons as their main tools of persuasion. IWW songs, which were included in the *Little Red Songbook* that many Wobblies carried, poked fun at the bosses and religious leaders and emphasized solidarity and class consciousness. Songs like Joe Hill's "The Preacher and the Slave" and Pat Kelly's "Hallelujah, I'm a Bum" used catchy melodies and simple lyrics to glorify the working class and illustrate the absurdity of offering an unreachable "pie in the sky" to hungry people. The inclusive policy and simple message of the IWW made it a very popular organization among the most downtrodden workers. The popularity of the IWW scared the employing and ruling classes; its militancy and confrontational style put the employers on the defensive. Through the nineteenth century, American employers had taken a very hard line on worker organizing, and there had been several violent episodes across the country as well as in Portland. Against heavy odds and hard opposition, the labor movement had established itself solidly in Portland by 1900, and with the revolutionary IWW at the forefront, it seemed to be on the verge of expanding its power.

At the beginning of the twentieth century, Portland had a well-established ruling/employing class made up of several prominent families descended from the city's early merchants. These families built great fortunes through real estate transactions and trading in the wide variety of goods and resources that poured into Portland from the surrounding countryside. Descendants of Ladd, Corbett, Failing, Ainsworth and their numerous friends made up the ruling class, as well as the membership of the Arlington Club. For half a century, the city had been organized and run for their benefit. While being descended from one of the "founding families" was important for social status, power was available to anyone who could accumulate enough money while maintaining a public image of respectability and virtue. Keeping up the appearance of respectability and virtue was not easy because most of the city's fortunes were at least partially based on the sale of alcohol and other vices and extreme exploitation of the working classes. The Progressive movement had risen up to combat the corrupt city government and thoroughly compromised police and judicial systems that had grown accustomed to serving the founding families. Their successes threatened the benefit that these families received from the corrupt system, and they were ready to use all the power available to them to protect it.

The women's movement finally succeeded in its campaign for equal suffrage by forging a coalition that included women from all points of the political spectrum. From Dr. Marie Equi, an open lesbian, abortionist and radical who supported the aims of the IWW, to Hattie Redmond, a leader of the Woman's Christian Temperance Union (WCTU) who believed in uplifting her African American race by demonstrating firm family values and conservative political principles, women united to get the vote. Once they achieved the vote, women were anything but a united voting group.

One thing that many women and men agreed on was that democracy could be used to cure the ills of society. This progressive idea took the form of expanding democratic participation while at the same time restricting personal liberty through mistakes such as the Eugenics Law, first passed in 1913, and prohibition, which was enacted in 1914 and took effect in 1916. The Eugenics Law was a failed social experiment that made the State of Oregon sterilize more than 2,500 mentally retarded people, homosexual men and individuals identified as habitual criminals between 1917 and 1983. Prohibition banned the manufacture, sale or transportation of intoxicating beverages.

Prohibition put the brakes on social change through democratic action by increasing the power of the police, who were more committed to stamping out radicalism than alcohol use. Frustrated political energy was converted into cultural resistance that created the country's first large counterculture. Identifying with jazz music and seeing illegal bootleg whiskey as a symbol of rebellion, the younger generation reveled in defying convention and redefining gender roles and sexuality, long repressed by still lingering Victorian values. Bolstered by "scientific" theory, members of the new generation redefined their grandparents' prejudices into scientifically proven systems of male dominance and white supremacy. The Great War, which preceded prohibition in most of the country, created a wave of xenophobia and violence that helped reinforce those two principles of American history. The war also left a demoralized "lost generation" of people who felt that ideals and moral values had been proven false. Materialism and greed became the most important elements of the new morality as wealth became the sole means of determining success.

Prohibition was not only an element in creating the demoralization of the lost generation; it also became one of its most important means of self-expression. Prohibition and its resistance became the defining experience of the generation. Movie stars got busted with liquor—like Wallace Reid, who was arrested in Portland in 1921. Popular musicians, like Louis Armstrong, made jokes about liquor in their songs, and politicians like Mayor Jimmy Walker of New York City and Mayor "Our George" Baker of Portland openly drank while giving full-throated hypocritical support to the enforcement of prohibition laws. The zeal for social change, which brought Portland to the brink of revolution in 1913, was frustrated by the prevalent war hysteria and the Red Scare that followed and converted into cultural energy. The lost generation produced some of the country's greatest artists, writers and musicians. From Sinclair Lewis to F. Scott Fitzgerald, from Louis Armstrong to George Gershwin, from D.W. Griffith to John Ford, the lost generation made a huge contribution to American culture.

It was the first age of mass ideology and identity as well. National products were starting to appear on store shelves all over the country, and their advertisement promoted national magazines that began to create a mass cultural identity for Americans. National magazines such as the *Saturday Evening Post*, which enjoyed the widest circulation and lasted longer than any of its rivals, except *Reader's Digest*, which continues today, told us what Americans thought about. Promoting patriarchy and Protestant religion, these magazines spread ideas and values across the country. Technological advances led to the availability of radio broadcasting, which was used even more effectively to promote ideas nationally. Cinema, still in its early stages, had already become an effective medium for changing ideas across the country. The film *Birth of a Nation* (1914) is one of the most important factors in the resurgence and renewed focus of the Ku Klux Klan in this period. The growing popularity of automobiles, which had been popular in Portland since at least 1905 but only for the rich, created a faster-moving, more mobile community that provided easy social anonymity. The spread of new ideas and the new mobility of the community led to a breakdown in moral values. Where their grandparents had been happy hypocrites, pretending the highest moral values while secretly indulging in vice, this new generation was haunted by the idea that morality meant nothing. Searching for escape, they looked back to the exciting days of yesteryear and idolized the so-called bad men of the American West. Harry Tracy, a small-time armed robber with a penchant for jail breaks, became the king of the Oregon bad men. Bootleggers soon took on the bad man mystique, and characters like Smitty the Bootlegger and Birdlegs Reed became local legends.

Prohibition had a major influence on Portland between 1916 and 1933, but there are two questions that have not been examined. How did prohibition come into effect in Oregon before the rest of the country? How were the prohibition laws enforced in Portland? Portland had a unique experience with prohibition. In many cities, such as Seattle, Chicago and New York, criminals were able to gain control of parts of the city government. Prohibition laws were difficult to enforce, and the money that could be made from breaking them could create a terrible temptation for law enforcement. Mayor Baker of Portland was elected in 1917, one year into prohibition. He saw the trouble the city had in trying to enforce the law, and he liked to drink with his friends. His unique plan was to take control of bootlegging in the city. Through police chief Leon Jenkins, the Portland police bureau took control of liquor distribution, and only the approved speakeasies that made regular payments and avoided violence as much as possible were allowed to operate.

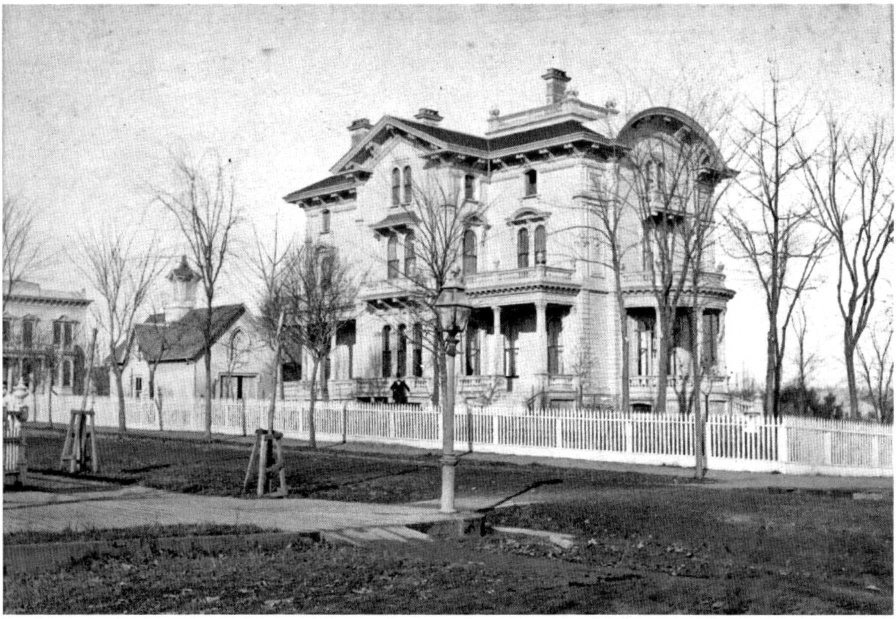

The Corbett Mansion, across the street from the Pioneer Courthouse, remained until the 1930s as a symbol of the old Portland that changed significantly during the years of prohibition (1916–33). Attorney Burl Green called it the "million-dollar cowbarn" and used it to illustrate Portland's provincialism. *Portland City Archive.*

Special squads of "secret police" worked to ferret out anyone who tried to compete with the official system, and a "raiding squad" seized their alcohol and closed them down. The alcohol stored in the Central Precinct basement became the main storehouse for booze and the mayor's liquor cabinet. Portland became the center of distribution of bonded liquor throughout the region, and the city maintained a reputation as the driest in the country, where liquor cost more than anywhere on the coast. But how did it all start?

By the nineteenth century, alcohol consumption had become a serious problem for the working class in America. In 1830, the average American consumed eighty-eight bottles of whiskey per year, more than three times the average consumption of today's drinker. Alcoholism was a problem that affected all classes, but the working class was especially vulnerable to the social problems associated with heavy drinking, which included poverty, domestic violence, child abuse and poor health. Followers of the "social gospel"—clergymen who saw it as a Christian duty to work for the betterment of society—soon made connections between these social ills and drinking and began to agitate against "demon rum" in a movement that became known as the temperance movement.

Temperance preachers, such as Reverend Thomas Lamb Eliot of Portland's First Unitarian Church, not only preached against the evils of booze, but they also urged their parishioners to fight against it. In the early decades of the nineteenth century, cities began to control the liquor trade with licenses and restrictive laws. In 1846, Maine became the first state in the union to ban alcohol, and by 1851 Maine was a completely dry state. Despite the problems associated with enforcement of prohibition—new words such as "rumrunner" and "bootlegger" came into popular use in Maine—many temperance activists dreamed of and worked for national Prohibition.

Portland's first temperance drive started as soon as the city was founded in 1851. Organized by Baptist and Methodist clergy, the movement was not popular in the newborn city, and alcohol prohibition, or even control, remained a fringe issue. In the 1870s, the women's movement, beginning in Ohio, took on the issue of temperance and inspired women all over the country to work for alcohol prohibition. The Women's Temperance Prayer League (WPTL) opened a Portland chapter in 1874, and a high-profile campaign against saloons began.

The struggle against the Webfoot and other popular saloons included civil disobedience and several arrests, but soon the activists learned that it was

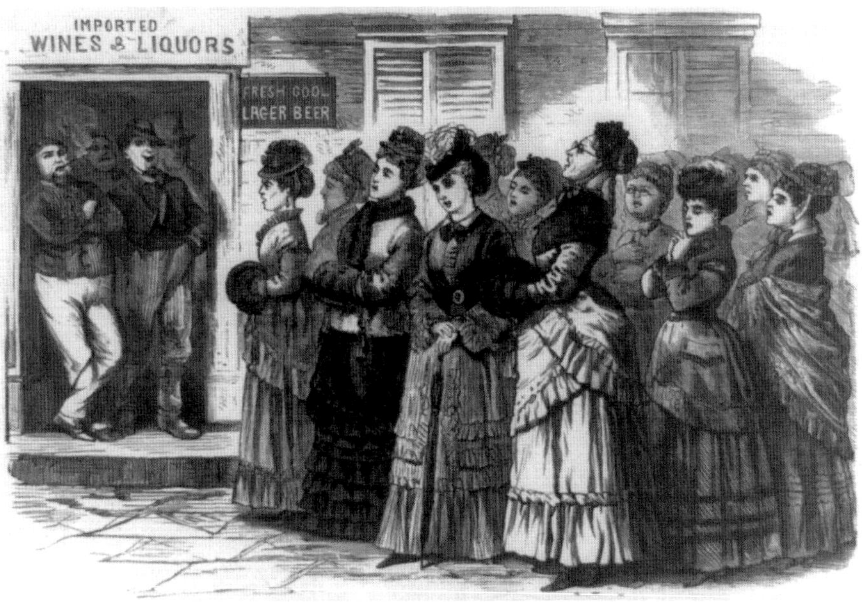


The Women's Temperance Prayer League, formed in 1874, was one of the first women's groups in Portland. Their direct-action campaign against saloons included civil disobedience and mass arrests. *From* Harper's Magazine. *U.S. Library of Congress.*

impossible to do anything against the entrenched liquor interests as long as women were not allowed to vote. By 1874, the "liquor interests" were well entrenched in Portland. James Lappeus, the chief of the new police department, was part owner of the Oro Fino Theater and Gem Saloon, the town's highest-class drinking and gambling establishment. William S. Ladd, Henry Corbett and the powerful Caples family were just a few members of Portland's elite who made at least part of their fortunes from the liquor trade. Portland had a saloon for every forty residents, and about half of the city's revenue came from liquor licenses. Abigail Scott Duniway pointed out in the *New Northwest* that the first prayers that would be answered for the temperance ladies would be answered when they had "ballots in their hands."

Soon, the WPTL folded itself into the national Woman's Christian Temperance Union (WCTU), and most of the temperance activists also became activists for women's suffrage. The long relationship between temperance and women's suffrage was a rocky one. Abigail Scott Duniway, Oregon's leading women's suffrage activist, blamed the temperance movement for the many defeats of women's suffrage at the ballot box. Many temperance activists felt that the struggle for the vote delayed prohibition until 1914. The split over these two issues pitted conservative feminists against radical feminists, and by the time women were finally allowed to vote (1913), the women's movement was badly divided with rivaling factions.

In 1887, Oregon voters defeated a proposed amendment to the state constitution that would have outlawed the production or sale of liquor. Even with its defeat at the polls, prohibition was not a dead letter in Oregon. The high consumption of alcohol and its association with poverty, domestic violence and poor health made temperance an important issue for many women. The WCTU continued to flourish and opened chapters all over the state. Its "home protection" campaign resonated strongly with conservative feminists and gained a great deal of support from clergy and other men who identified themselves as being "dry."

The National Anti-Saloon League (ASL), later known as the Anti-Saloon League of America, was founded in Ohio in 1893. In 1895, it went national with its "local option" campaign, which allowed cities and counties to individually vote on prohibition. The ASL was an electoral, nonpartisan organization that endorsed candidates for office who supported prohibition, regardless of their party. It was the first single-issue pressure group in American politics, and it set a pattern for decades to come. The ASL began forming chapters in Oregon in 1903 and found fertile ground here.

# CHAPTER 1
# PROHIBITION

*You can't cure thirst by law.*
*—John Kobler*

As the clock counted down to midnight on December 31, 1915, Portland was getting ready to launch one of its most radical social experiments. At 12:01 a.m. it would become illegal in Oregon to make, sell, barter, give away or transport intoxicating liquor. Portland's many drinking establishments were jam-packed as thirsty revelers indulged in what might be their last drink and celebration reigned. In the North End, where transients gathered, and in South Portland, where immigrant families were crowded, mourning seemed more in order. By morning there would be a small rash of suicides as desperate alcoholics contemplated a dry future.

George Luis Baker, former theater manager and current city commissioner, was looking forward to the new era. He was already making plans to run for mayor in 1917 and was busily imagining the Portland that he would shape. Anna Schrader, a young woman with a troubled past, had recently married for the second time and was making plans to be the fire department candidate for Rose Queen in the spring. The insecure woman from rural Minnesota was trying desperately to get the attention of her new city. Leon Jenkins, a veteran of seven years in the Portland Police Bureau, was night-shift supervisor and eager for opportunities to advance his career. Lola Baldwin, Portland's first female police officer and founder of the Women's Protective Division, was on the verge of national recognition for her work. A strict teetotaler and prohibition supporter, her New Year's celebration was dry and ended early. Floyd Marsh, a young miner from Arizona, was still working his way toward Portland through Gold Beach and the Rogue River gold country. Tom Johnson, an African American ex–armed robber, hosted a roaring party at the Orpheus Club in the North End. He was still trying to figure out where his liquor would come from the next day. Bobby Evans, a boxer from South Portland, was reevaluating his career. After years of hitting and being hit, Evans was planning his new career as a boxing promoter. A hustler since the days he sold newspapers on the street, Evans was never one to let a good opportunity go by, legal or not. Dr. Marie Equi, a young doctor and open lesbian, was devoting more and more of her time to her work among the poor and unemployed. She thought liquor was evil because it made the working class less revolutionary. She welcomed prohibition, but not the Red Scare that came with it. And at Birdlegs' Union Club in the North Park blocks, music and laughter reigned. Some of Portland's earliest jazz performances were at the Union Club, and its owner, a blind African American man named James "Birdlegs" Reed, already knew where his liquor would be coming from the next day.

Lola Baldwin and her fellow prohibitionists had taken a long road to get to this day. In some ways, their sense of victory was akin to that women felt when they won the vote in 1912. The method used to pass the prohibition law, however, changed the political landscape in Oregon, as it eventually would across the country. The temperance movement had always been a moral movement and only rarely had the support of politicians before the Anti-Saloon League. The ASL brought politics and politicians to the movement. It built membership and raised funds through the congregations of churches that supported its issue. Church members provided a strong grass-roots base that gave the organization power at the ballot box. The newly instituted "Oregon System," which included the citizens' initiative, provided new opportunities for electoral campaigns. In 1904, the Local Option Act was passed in Oregon, and the ASL began organizing dry initiatives in communities all over the state. In 1905, Hood River became the first Oregon city to outlaw liquor, and soon the state was dotted with dry counties.

Ambitious, progressive political activists were attracted to the ASL, where they could gain electoral experience and often become candidates for office themselves. In Oregon, one of the most important ASL activists was E.S.J. McAllister, a young graduate of the University of Virginia, who left a failed marriage and moved to Portland in 1904. As legal counsel for the ASL's

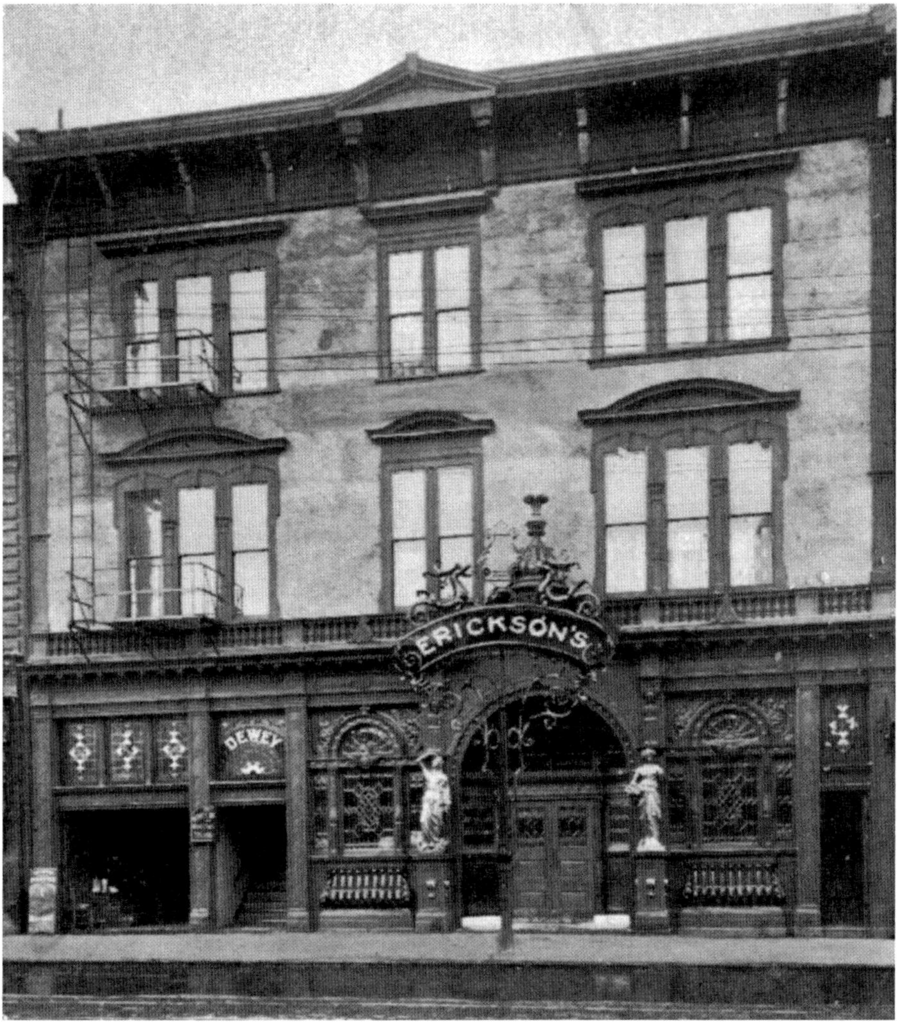


A workingman's club known as Erickson's was legendary all over the West for the world's longest bar. Saloons like Erickson's were more than just bars; they were the center of social life for their communities and served many economic functions besides selling liquor. *Portland City Archive.*

Southern Oregon and Idaho Departments, McAllister traveled all over the region organizing ASL chapters and making political enemies. In Portland, he became a powerful ally of the Progressive Party and was elected president of the People's Forum, a popular program of debate and political education that included such important figures as Abigail Scott Duniway, C.E.S. Wood and William U'Ren. All the time McAllister was building a promising political career he was leading a double life, as he entered into life partnership with Roy Kadel and became an influential member of Portland's underground gay community.

Portland's gay community was divided strictly by gender and class. Lesbians, such as Dr. Marie Equi, were accepted into the community fairly easily. Although Dr. Equi stirred up a scandal when she was unsuccessfully sued by the parents of one of her lovers for "corrupting" the girl and her radical politics raised many eyebrows, her "Boston Marriage" lifestyle was winked at. Dr. Equi and her partner even adopted a daughter who called Equi "Da." Equi was the most open and vocal lesbian in town, but other women lived together as "spinsters," and few people ever questioned, or wondered about, their sexual orientation.

Working-class men who engaged in same-sex sexual relationships enjoyed anonymity to some degree as well. Except for periodic "moral crusades," sexual activity between working-class men was largely ignored. Most Oregonians before 1912 understood homosexuality in terms of Max Nordau's theory of "degeneration": since the working class was a degenerated class, it was expected that they would engage in "unnatural acts." Historian Peter Boag estimated that as many as 70 percent of the transient workers who dominated Oregon's labor force engaged in same-sex affairs. In Portland, the "wide open" North End provided several hotels, saloons and pool halls where men could meet for sexual purposes. Middle-class and upper-class gay men, on the other hand, had to keep their sexual orientation strictly hidden or they could face terrible consequences.

E.S.J. McAllister, and many others like him, was forced to live a double life, and an underground gay culture developed. The Imperial Hotel on Southwest Twelfth Avenue was the center of the secret gay culture downtown, with the basement men's room often used for sexual liaisons. Around the hotel a small colony of gay-owned businesses grew. The ABC Restaurant, owned by Claude Bronner, and E.S.J. McAllister's Smart Shop Millinery Store were among the businesses that catered to a gay clientele. Using secret code words and clothing signals, the business owners and their customers kept their gay identity a closely guarded secret. Among this class, the exposure of a man's secrets could result in losing everything.

The 1912 vice clique scandal exposed the secrets of Portland's hidden gay community, and several men lost everything. It began with the arrest of a young male prostitute who quickly revealed extensive homosexual activity at the downtown YMCA. One of Portland's earliest and biggest sex scandals soon exploded in lurid headlines on the front page of the *Portland Telegram*

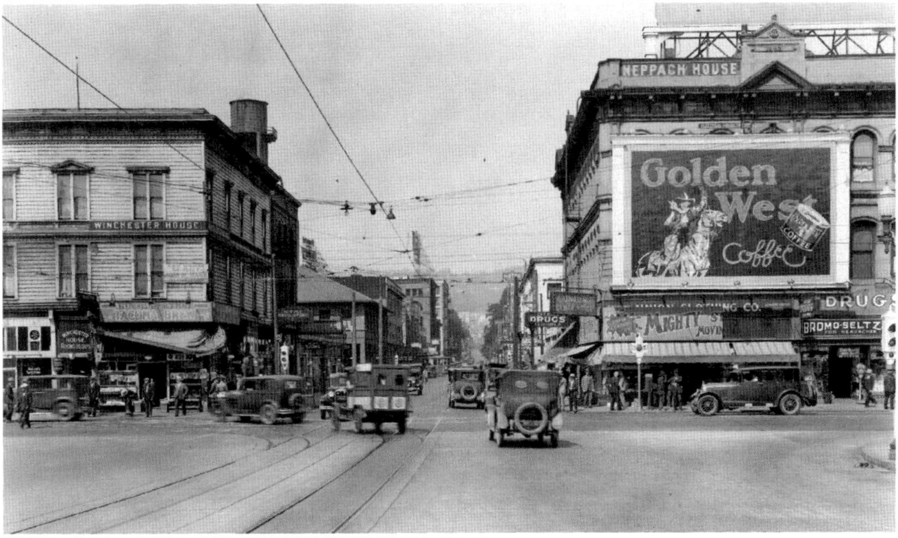


West Burnside Street as it looked before the street was widened in 1933. This neighborhood has always been known for its transient hotels and drinking establishments. *Portland City Archive.*

and other papers. The lives of several men were ruined, both socially and financially. Dr. Harry Start was convicted of sodomy and faced two to five years in prison. Although his conviction was overturned on appeal, Dr. Start found Portland to be an uncomfortable town, and he fled, going into exile in China. William H. Allen, a Spanish-American War veteran, chose suicide rather than face trial for sodomy. Claude Bronner cooperated with the police and gave evidence against several of his friends but still served nearly five years in prison after being convicted.

E.S.J. McAllister's conviction on sodomy charges was overturned on a technicality, but the exposure of his relationships with Kadel and others cost him nearly everything. His promising political career in shambles, McAllister resigned from the People's Forum. Publicly humiliated, he fled to Myrtle Creek in rural Douglas County, where he lived out the rest of his short life in anonymity. Many Portlanders were shocked to learn that several prominent men enjoyed sex with other men, and an anti-gay attitude prevailed in Portland until well into the 1980s. One of the first manifestations of this new attitude was the passage of the 1913 Eugenics Law, which called for castrating men convicted of sodomy, among others.

Despite sex scandal in Portland and allegations of financial and ethical irregularity among ASL staff in several cities, the Anti-Saloon League continued to build support for alcohol prohibition. In 1912, the same year as the vice clique scandal, women finally achieved the right to vote in Oregon. Wets—who opposed alcohol prohibition—feared that the newly enfranchised women would try to take away their booze. It was not a baseless fear. The Anti-Saloon League began planning for a statewide prohibition initiative, but in 1913, the fight was still city by city. The prohibition fight in 1913 didn't go well for the ASL; only Hillsboro and Milwaukie voted to go dry, while several other cities defeated "dry" initiatives. The vote was so close in Milwaukie (a margin of about forty votes) that accusations of voter fraud flew both ways.

The dismal results at the polls didn't discourage organizers for the ASL or the WCTU, and in November 1914 statewide initiative 332 gave the voters of Oregon the chance to vote on the prohibition of alcohol. It was a hard-fought election, with the "liquor interests" spending thousands of dollars to defeat the initiative, especially in Multnomah County. The ASL and WCTU spent money, too, but they also concentrated on grass-roots organizing among church congregations. Their "get out the vote" effort swept the polls on election day; voter turnout records were broken as about 80 percent of eligible voters cast ballots. The prohibition initiative passed in every county but one. The wets had hoped for a large vote in Multnomah County that could overwhelm the rural vote from the rest of the state, but when the ballots had been counted, prohibition passed in Multnomah County by about three hundred votes. Clatsop County was the only one in the state that voted down prohibition and only by a margin of thirty votes. When all the counting was done, prohibition passed in Oregon by more than twenty-four thousand votes. It would be up to the state legislature to pass laws for enforcing the ban, but as of January 1, 1916, most liquor would be illegal in Oregon.

With help from the ASL, which also worked as a lobbying group, the state legislature passed the Anderson Act in 1915. This act made it illegal to make, sell or barter intoxicating liquor except for medicinal, mechanical, scientific or sacramental reasons, all of which required a prescription from a licensed pharmacist. The act didn't attempt to deal with the importation of alcohol, which was still a controversial issue, except to limit the amount of liquor that an Oregonian could import for personal use. The Anderson Act, like all of the other prohibition acts that would follow, had a fatal flaw: it only illegalized the supply of alcohol; it did nothing to address the demand. For example, although it was illegal to make, sell or barter a bottle of whiskey, it was not illegal to own or drink it. In fact, under the Anderson Act, an

Oregonian could legally import up to twenty-four quarts of malt liquor or two quarts of wine or "spirituous liquor," which included whiskey, for personal use every month.

Predictions about the economic effects of prohibition were dire. The *Oregonian* predicted a drop in municipal revenues of more than $340,000 when liquor licenses stopped being renewed in December 1915. The paper predicted tax increases of as much as $170,000 for 1916. In the North End, many drunks trembled at the idea of the booze drying up. A citizens' group urged the city to provide treatment for delirium tremens—withdrawal from alcohol, also known as "the DTs"—which was common among the derelicts of Burnside Street, near the red-light district. Larry Sullivan, the sailors' boardinghouse man and political boss of the North End, just smiled at the new law and made plans to continue selling liquor through his "roadhouses" strategically placed just outside city jurisdiction. James "Birdlegs" Reed also smiled at the law. His Union Club in northwest Portland would be the scene of Portland's first "liquor raid" in January 1916, but Reed had cleverly hidden any evidence of alcohol in the place and the police were frustrated in their efforts. It would not be the last run-in between Birdlegs and the Portland police.

When Oregon went dry, the legal importation of liquor didn't amount to much. In February, about 1,200 people ordered liquor from out of state for personal use; by November, nearly 35,000 were taking advantage of the convenient loophole. Washington went dry at the same time Oregon did, so California and British Columbia benefitted from liquor sales. In the first days of prohibition, the Southern Pacific Railroad, which made regular runs between Oakland, California, and Portland, became the most reliable pipeline of high-quality booze. Pullman porters, all African American men just beginning the secret organizing campaign that would result in A. Phillip Randolph's Brotherhood of Sleeping Car Porters, used their imagination and ingenuity to make sure that their passengers could always get a drink in the dining and lounge cars. Branching out from this flow, young black men, such as John Lowe, Sam "Yam" Wallace and Lawrence Tucker, and women, such as Lucile Simelton, helped to keep the bonded liquor flowing to the clubs of northwest Portland, which now operated behind locked doors and often required secret passwords for entry. Leadership would change as the founders of the "Pullman Porter Ring" each met his own brand of bad luck, but under the new leadership, the operation would continue to supply Portland's "after hours" clubs with high-quality, tax-free liquor well into the 1950s.

The Anderson Act did little to stop the flow of liquor into Oregon. The Multnomah County Sheriff's Office first took responsibility for enforcement, and in a decision that set the pattern for prohibition enforcement, it decided to focus on bootlegging in the African American community. George Hardin had recently become the first black sheriff's deputy, and he was eager to go after bootleggers. Hardin went undercover at the Golden West Hotel and began to document the activities of John Lowe and hotel manager Al Green. He made several arrests of Pullman porters near the hotel, but they were mostly for possession of a small flask or, at most, a quart of whiskey. It would be a little while before Sheriff Thomas Hurlburt could move against the Golden West, but it was becoming clear that liquor was flowing from the Southern Pacific Railroad, through Union Depot, to the Golden West and the Victoria Hotels.

In 1916, H. Russell Albee was nearing the end of his term as mayor and was probably looking forward to retirement. Albee had been elected in 1913, the first mayor of Portland's new commission government, which had been put in place to end the decades of corrupt "ward politics" that had ruled since the 1870s. Elected as a Progressive, Albee tried to focus on issues he felt were important: riverfront improvement, garbage collection and transit rates. Instead, he was put on the defensive by events, and his administration lurched from crisis to crisis. Blamed for not being tough enough on vice or on radicals, Albee sometimes had police chief John Clark stage high-publicity vice raids to distract the public. By 1916, the mayor had survived two recall elections and one revolt by the city council. With pressure mounting from the ASL, WCTU and the Law and Order League (LOL), a vigilante group that formed in reaction to the 1901 assassination of William McKinley and had been organizing in Multnomah County since 1907, to enforce the prohibition law, Mayor Albee ordered John Clark to act.

Clark had been police chief since the beginning of Albee's term in 1913 and had a long career as chief of St. Paul, Minnesota's police force and head of security for the Great Northern Railroad. By 1916, he had been a police officer for more than forty years. In response to Mayor Albee's order, Clark formed a "morals squad" under the leadership of Lieutenant Leo A. Harms, a veteran of war in the Philippines and the city's first police lieutenant. The morals squad was to enforce the alcohol laws, as well as laws against prostitution and gambling, activities often associated with drinking in Portland clubs. Harms inaugurated his new squad with a raid on a "blind pig"—an illegal drinking joint—on Northwest Twelfth Avenue. The morals squad swooped down on the run-down boardinghouse and arrested Lucile Simelton and Lawrence Tucker with nine quarts of whiskey—knowing their connections, it was the good stuff. The charge against Tucker was thrown out and a jury refused to convict Simelton, but the raid was something that both the mayor and the chief could point to. It seemed as if both the mayor and the chief were wearing out. Law enforcement became a big issue in the election of 1917, and city commissioner George L. Baker, a candidate for mayor, made the most of it. No one would ever charge Baker with being soft on crime or on radicals.

# CHAPTER 2
# THE GIRL RUSH

*The average working girl is lamentably ignorant and innocent of the ways of the tempter, whether he appears clothed in a dress suit or rough homespun.*
*–Lola Baldwin*

Wearing large hats and sheltered from the hot sun by umbrellas, eager crowds gathered by the Columbia Court of the Lewis and Clark Centennial Exposition at Lakeview Terrace on July 6, 1905, to witness the unveiling of the bronze statue of Sacagawea, the Shoshone Indian woman who assisted the Lewis and Clark Expedition of 1805. The beautiful statue, which can still be seen in Washington Park, was sculpted by Alice Cooper, one of the first female American artists to work in cast bronze. The event came the day after the end of the thirty-seventh annual National American Woman Suffrage Association (NAWSA) conference that had brought feminists from all over the state and all over the country to plan strategy for winning the vote for women. Portland was chosen for the national convention for two reasons: the hope women had for winning a Woman Suffrage Initiative campaign that would be on the ballot in 1906 and the Lewis and Clark Centennial Exposition that brought thousands of people swarming to Portland from all over the region. Eighty-six-year-old Susan B. Anthony, in one of the last public appearances of her life, sat on the platform next to her old friend and rival Abigail Scott Duniway, who had been leading the fight for women's votes in Oregon since the 1870s. In the audience, young Lola Baldwin, working as an agent of the YMCA

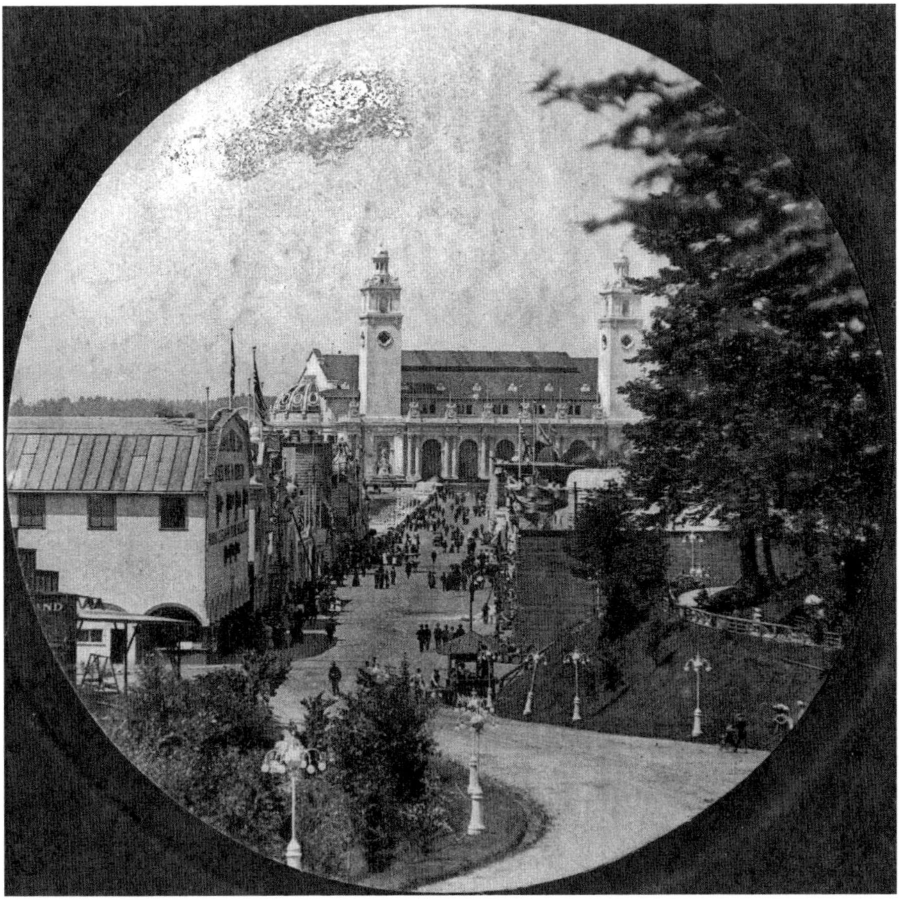

The 1905 Lewis and Clark Exposition greatly stimulated Portland's population growth. Between 1905 and 1910, the population grew from 160,000 to over 270,000, and it had doubled by 1920. A good percentage of the new Portlanders were women. *Portland City Archive.*

Traveler's Aid Association, scanned the crowd looking for predatory men and unaccompanied young women. Baldwin always had a nose for radicals, and she probably kept her eye on young Dr. Marie Equi, a recent graduate of the OSU Medical School and an open lesbian who had not yet woken to her commitment to radical politics.

Dr. Harry Lane, Portland's beloved "people's doctor" and recently elected mayor, took the stage and gave one of his most memorable and moving speeches. Mayor Lane, grandson of Oregon's first governor and Indian fighter extraordinaire Joseph Lane, took the opportunity to explain that any form of violence between white and native populations had occurred because of "white people ill-treating the Indians who had befriended them." In his speech, he also called for an annual "festival of roses," an idea that took root with Portland's first Rose Festival in 1907. Dr. Lane was a good choice of speaker for the women's event. As mayor, he would lead the country in the appointment of women to public office, including Sarah Evans, the young woman who had taken the leading hand in organizing the Sacagawea event.

Sacagawea had become an important symbol to the women's movement since the 1902 publication of *The Conquest: The True Story of Lewis and Clark* by Eva Emery Dye. The novel focused on the adventures of the "little bird woman" who saved the expedition from starvation and being lost several times on the trip. Susan B. Anthony and Abigail Scott Duniway, when it was their turn to speak, both made connections between the Indian woman who was the first woman to vote in Oregon, at Fort Clatsop in 1806, and the need for women's votes.

The unveiling of the Sacagawea statue was one of the headline events of Portland's 1905 Lewis and Clark Exposition. The idea for a world's fair originally germinated in the mind of a dry goods merchant named Dan McAllen. At a meeting of local business leaders in 1885, McAllen suggested that the city could use the added commerce that a world's fair would generate, urging "that Portland mark the new century and pull itself out of its economic slump by holding some sort of international fair." One of the first challenges of the 1905 Lewis and Clark Exposition had been to find an appropriate theme that would be catchy and appealing. The primary impetus for the world's fair was strictly financial, but to make the event attractive to locals and out-of-state travelers, there had to be a theme. In time, the Oregon Historical Society was instrumental in solving the problem, suggesting that the centennial anniversary of the 1805 Lewis and Clark Expedition's sojourn in Oregon would be a suitable event to commemorate. With that problem solved, a motto had to be decided on as well, in an effort to increase publicity and add to the fun of anticipated festivities. The motto eventually became "Westward the Course of Empire Takes Its Way."

The wealthy and affluent men of Portland were determined to create a memorable event, unequaled in its style, elegance and profitability. The initial stages were difficult, though, as this included purchasing and securing exhibits and arranging for more investors to take an interest. Portland companies like Henry Weinhard Brewing invested, along with the Ladd and Tilton Bank and the Northern Pacific Railroad. In addition to wealthy local businessmen, approximately three thousand ordinary Portland citizens purchased stock certificates to support and invest in what they felt would be a promising venture.

The location for the fairgrounds was chosen with care, as the organizers wanted a scene of serene, elegant beauty. Northwest Portland's Guilds Lake evaporated during the hot summer months and remained at a depth of only two and a half feet during the rest of the year. It was chosen as the ideal site for the fairgrounds since it was not too deep and would present no real danger to small children, pets or the elderly. It was located near the recently constructed Vaughn Street Park, which hosted baseball games and other events. The stadium would be useful to the workers during the operation of the fair and would assist with food storage, shelter from the hot sun and a needed respite from long working hours.

The site was also convenient because it was located near the residential area of northwest Portland and could be accessible for nearly all Portlanders. The site was easy to get to from the river, with local steamers charging ten cents a ride, and by streetcar as well. The low-cost buildings, clearly not meant to last and made cheaply of plaster over wood frames, were designed in the style of the Spanish Renaissance, adding to the romantic beauty of the site. The domed white Agricultural Palace personified this ideal most of all. It sat before 406 acres of marble statuary and elegant landscaping. All the buildings were created with numerous flourishes, such as the traditional red-tiled roofs, domes and a multitude of cupolas and arched doorways. The Gothic architecture lent an entirely romantic appearance to the buildings, adding to the scenic beauty and to the sense of Portland as an up-and-coming cultural center of some significance. Along with the main exhibits, there was an amusement park for children and young adults, blimp rides, classical music concerts, sideshows and free motion pictures, which were in the infancy of their development. There were also endless vendors selling hot food and lemonade to the curious crowds of wandering spectators.

Part of the need to create the 1905 Centennial Exposition came from the fact that many in town felt the population was too low. In the early days and all through the middle and late 1800s, more men came to Portland than women. In 1905, there were still about five men for every woman in Portland. Local citizens and businessmen wanted a more diverse population of Americans to come to Oregon from out of state. They wanted new people to set down roots and add to the growth and industry, and a four-month-long world's fair would accomplish that feat nicely.

The Lewis and Clark Exposition was very successful at stimulating population growth. Between 1905 and 1910, Portland's population grew from 161,000 to over 270,000 and had doubled by 1920. A good percentage of the new Portlanders were women in what amounted to a "Girl Rush."

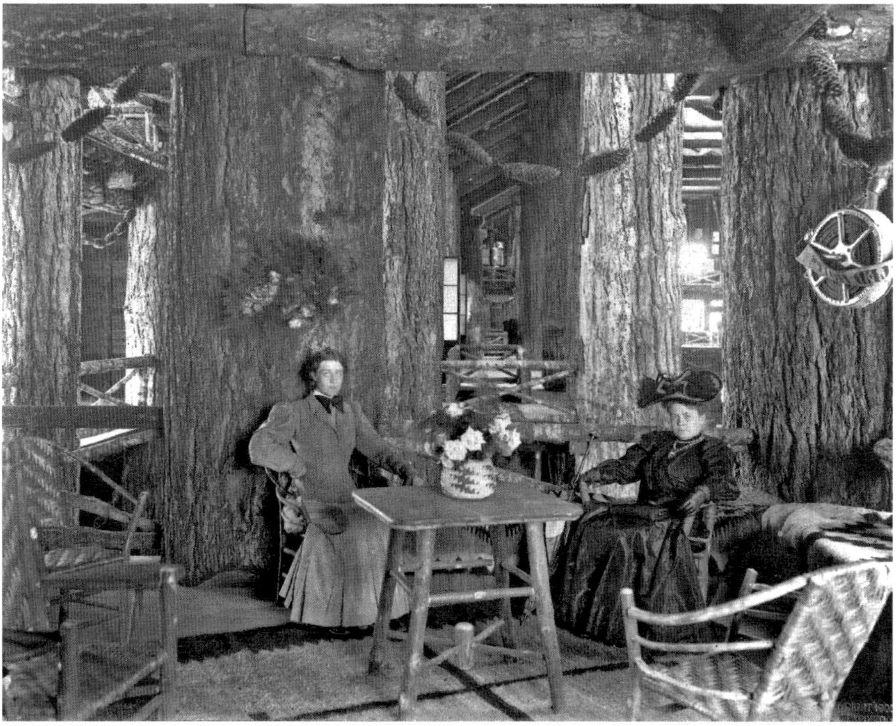

These women are enjoying the mezzanine of the Expo's Forestry Center, which glorified Oregon's lumber industry. Most of the women who came to Portland found good opportunities; some of them found danger. *Portland City Archive.*

In 1905, more than 1,700 young women made Portland their home. That trickle soon became a flood, and by 1907 more than 7,000 women a year were coming to Portland looking for new lives. Opportunities were excellent for women whether they sought a husband or a career as Portland transformed itself into a bustling city with a lively economy. Transportation was the bedrock of Portland's economy as agricultural products, especially wheat, lumber and minerals from the Columbia Plateau and the Willamette Valley, poured into the city, and the Southern Pacific, Northern Pacific and Union Pacific Railroads and countless steamships transported those goods to points all over the world.

During the growth and increased commerce of the city, a number of groups, businesses and societies formed to celebrate Portland. Some of these groups are now enjoying their own centennials and contribute to the civic pride that has always been a part of the Portland identity and spirit. Some of the groups that have made it to the hundred-year mark are the Arlington Club, Huber's Café, the Jantzen Swimwear Company, the Linnton Lumber Company, the Rotary Club, Reynolds Optical, the Royal Rosarians and the influential Commission of Public Docks.

The women who came to Portland during the Girl Rush were from all over the country, small towns and large. For example, Beatrice Morrow came from a small town in Texas by way of Chicago in 1912; Louise Bryant came from Reno, Nevada, and moved to Portland after graduating from the University of Oregon in 1909; Anna Schrader came to Portland from the rural town of Medalia, Minnesota, in 1910. From all over the country they came to Portland looking for a job, an adventure or a husband; what they all wanted was a new life. Many of them found what they were looking for; some of them found more than they bargained for. Though women earned less than half of what men earned, these newcomers, dressed in long woolen skirts and large, elaborate hats, benefited from the work, culture and optimism they found in Oregon.

Opportunities for women were exploding in Portland. If a woman was looking for a husband, there were so many single men available that nothing could be easier. If she was looking for a job, there were more new opportunities than ever before. Where her mother had been limited to employment as a teacher, shop girl or laundress, with a few of the most adventurous going into professional careers, for the modern girl, options seemed almost unlimited.

Healthcare was a good option. By 1905, Oregon already had more than three times as many female doctors per capita as any other state in the nation. Dr. Bethenia Owens Adair, who pioneered as a doctor in the 1870s, was still practicing in Astoria. Dr. Esther Pohl Lovejoy, Dr. Marie Equi and Dr. Alys Griff were just the most visible doctors with thriving practices, and women's health was already a recognized specialty. Sarah Evans was a pioneer woman in journalism, working as the editor of the Women's Work page of the *Oregon Journal*. The *Oregonian* hired its first female reporter, Louise Bryant, in 1909. Mary Frances Isom, head librarian of the Portland Library Association, pioneered as a woman working in public service. Women were making their mark in business, education and many other fields. Mayor Harry Lane supported this process by appointing women to highly visible public positions. He appointed Esther Pohl Lovejoy as head of the Department of Public Health and Sarah Evans as market inspector. His most notable appointment came in 1908, when he hired Lola Baldwin as the city's first female police officer.

Lola Baldwin came to Portland in 1904 with her husband, who managed Portland's first national chain retail store. For many years, she worked as a volunteer with "wayward girls," and she devoted her life to helping and protecting young women. During the preparations for the Lewis and Clark Exposition, Baldwin lobbied tirelessly for a "protective service" to assist young women and children visitors. To demonstrate the need for such a service, Baldwin cited the fact that more than 1,100 young women had disappeared from world's fairs and expos in the twelve years since the Chicago Exposition. As a result, she was hired by the YMCA as head of the Travelers' Aid Association (TAA). She directed a small force of women who worked regular shifts on the fairgrounds to provide assistance to travelers in need, especially women and children. During the four months of the exposition, the women of the TAA provided assistance to more than 1,700 women who found themselves stranded without support in Portland or who were at risk of falling prey to the pimps, drug addicts and thieves who haunted the Trail looking for vulnerable victims.

The Trail, one of the biggest attractions of the expo, was a blocks-long midway lined with food vendors, exhibits, shooting galleries and attractions of all kinds. The Trail was the expo's version of an amusement park. Along with popcorn, peanuts and cold drinks, you could sample delicacies such as nougat candy and giant roast beef sandwiches. You could walk through the Mirror Maze, the Haunted Castle and the Temple of Mirth and view the world-famous Incubator Babies. There were thrilling rides like the Water Chutes, the Haunted Swing and the Blue Grotto. Exotic displays of living human beings, like the Filipino and Japanese Villages, the Old Plantation, the California Radium Experiment and the Siberian Railroad, thrilled crowds. For those with racier tastes, there was a "Glimpse of a Harem," Jabour's Gay Paree and the Streets of Cairo, where Little Egypt performed her notorious hoochie-coochie dance. There was something for everyone, and thousands visited the Trail, many of them coming back repeatedly through the summer. Lola Baldwin and the other Travelers' Aid agents spent much of their time watching the Trail and keeping track of the pimps and drug dealers who waited for unwary young women who could be turned into prostitutes.

Police chief Charles Hunt had warned that the expo would attract criminals from all over to prey on the crowds, and the police department had been expanded to meet the challenge. However, crime rose significantly during and after the expo, and the trend lasted for the rest of the century. The beefed-up police force was not well equipped to handle the problem. Until the 1930s, the main qualifications for police officers were strength and the ability to fight. While both are important qualities in police officers, they are not the only things needed. The lack of analytic and detection skills was especially evident among homicide detectives, and many of the murders committed during this era were never solved. In addition, Portland police officers were extremely low paid, and the force had a long tradition of "pay for service." Since the earliest days of policing in Portland, officers earned fees for providing services, such as killing and burying stray dogs, keeping the streets clean, collecting taxes and so forth. Night patrols were often paid by individual businesses, and officers on night shifts and "special officers" ignored law violations against businesses or citizens who wouldn't pay. In 1905, there were still many officers who had been on the force since the 1870s and 1880s, and they had transmitted this culture to the younger generation as they arrived. Many officers were open to the idea of "looking the other way" for payment; protecting vulnerable young women was not their highest priority. That was Lola Baldwin's job.

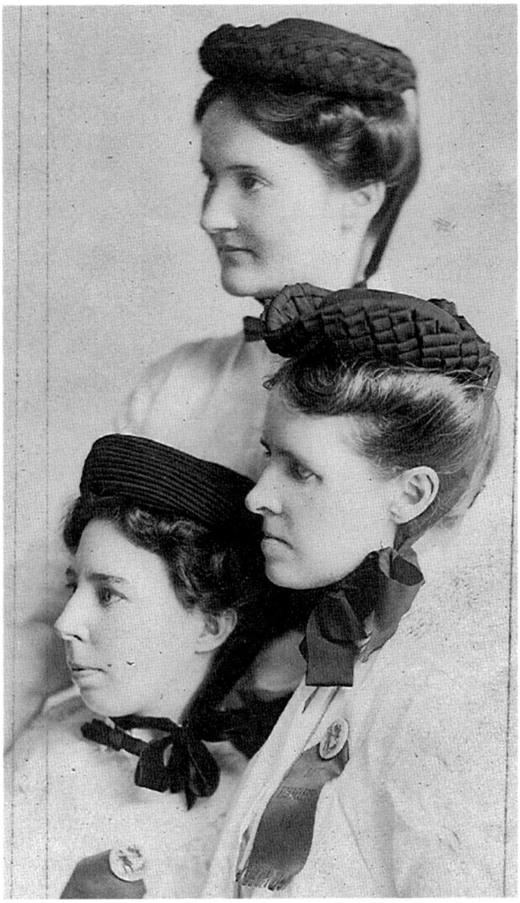

Members of the YMCA Travelers' Aid Association in 1905. *Top to bottom*: Grace E. Fix, Lola Baldwin and Dagmar Riley. *Portland Police Historical Society.*

The Travelers' Aid Association helped its charges with financial assistance, lodging, clothes, long-distance communication, job training and placement—whatever was needed to help women out of unsafe situations. There were some women who refused assistance and some they missed. The brothels downtown and in the North End did brisk business, but the work of the TAA was a godsend for many of the people it helped. Lola and her girls continued to work after the expo closed as long as they could find funding.

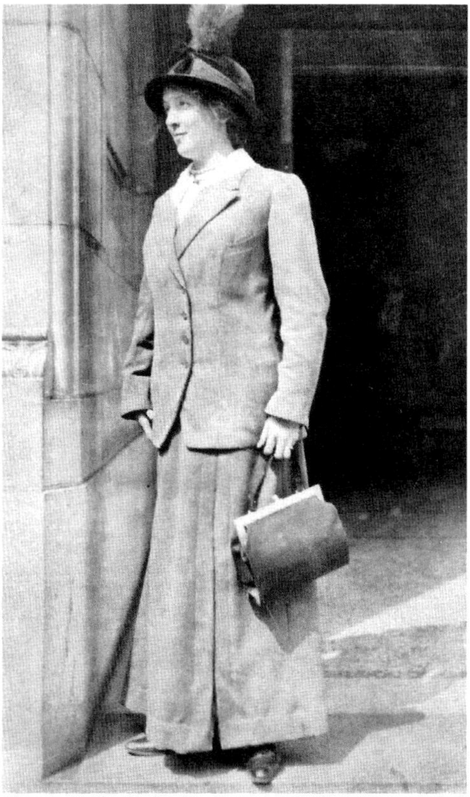

In 1908, Lola Baldwin set up the Women's Protective Division and over the next few years recruited a staff of female officers. Wilma Chandler (pictured) was one of these officers. Her badge and gun are concealed in her purse. The purse itself could serve as a nightstick. *Portland Police Historical Society.*

Baldwin lobbied Mayor Lane and the city council endlessly for funding until finally, in 1908, she was hired by the police bureau, becoming the nation's second female police officer. Marie Owens, the country's first female police officer, worked the streets of Chicago as a detective for a brief time in the 1890s.

In her thirteen-year career with the Portland Police Bureau, Lola Baldwin founded the Women's Protective Division (WPD), recruited and trained a staff of female officers, helped set up Portland's first juvenile justice system, helped start the Hillcrest School and assisted cities all over the West to set up Women's Protective Divisions and Juvenile Justice Systems. She gained national attention and during the Great War helped to police U.S. Army camps and hospitals. The whole time, she was a strong advocate for women's rights, crime prevention and vocational training for women.

Eventually, after only thirteen years on the job, Baldwin retired from the Portland Police Bureau in 1922 with a changed and, some might say, cynical perspective on life in general. She had become troubled by the changing social and cultural norms that had occurred after the Great War. She expressed disappointment and disapproval at what she viewed to be a disintegration of public and personal morality and integrity. Women smoking tobacco was one of many things she strongly disapproved of, as well as the significant increase in juvenile crime that she observed. She was also upset by the glamor and prestige of the "bad girl" or "flapper" style of attitude, appearance and demeanor that women seemed so eager to adopt in the early 1920s. She found she could not adapt to these new changes in American culture and retired from the police force early, profoundly disappointed in the ways the world was changing.

Mayor Harry Lane was one of Portland's unforgettable characters. A Democrat, Lane was born in Corvallis and was a rare breed of man in that he personified the original spirit of progressive reform that would plant its seeds in Portland and become firmly entrenched here. Lane had been a physician and public health advocate and was the grandson of Joseph Lane, Oregon's first territorial governor and also a U.S. senator. As a graduate of Willamette University Medical School in 1876, Lane went on to study in New York and Europe before setting up a medical practice in San Francisco and then, later, in Portland.

In 1887, Lane was hired by then governor Sylvester Pennoyer as the superintendent of the Oregon State Insane Asylum, known today as the Oregon State Hospital. Working at the hospital for less than four years, Lane discovered conditions of extreme abuse, neglect and administrative corruption. He aggressively put forth charges of corruption against the entire institution, contacting local Portland authorities and several important people. But to his dismay, he discovered that any accusations of corruption he made fell on deaf ears. Lane made many enemies in the hospital and elsewhere by attempting to provide disclosure of the horrible conditions and to improve them. He was in the wrong place at the wrong time. In 1891, Governor Pennoyer, bowing to pressure as he usually did, forced Lane to resign his position at the asylum so it could be taken over by someone less dedicated to social justice.

After resigning from his post at the insane asylum, Lane served on Oregon's first state board of health from 1903 to 1907. He became known as a man who worked hard to prevent disease, promoting public awareness of the dangers and prevention of tuberculosis, which was highly contagious and primarily impacted lower-income populations. Lane valued, understood and promoted the importance of protecting clean water and encouraging Oregonians to buy and grow good-quality food to sustain their families.

Throughout his entire medical career, he demonstrated a profound understanding of the social stressors of those less fortunate and how they struggled to overcome poverty and the indifference of the upper classes. Lane often didn't charge Portlanders in need, who had no way to pay for medical care. He quickly became known as the "poor people's doctor," developing a reputation as a man who cared and was beloved in those diverse Portland communities of low-income families.

In November 1912, Lane was elected to the U.S. Senate, the first time the office was filled by popular election, where he became a leading national advocate for women's suffrage. Fighting against women's "separatism" from society as a whole and promoting more equitable treatment of women was highly unusual for a man at this time. During his time in the Senate, Lane encouraged a more benevolent rapport between the U.S. government and the Native American population. He advocated support and health services for Native Americans that many others in the Senate simply did not value.

Although Lane served two two-year terms as Portland mayor and was a committed social reformer, he may have been born into the wrong time. He was up against a formidable structure of institutionalized city corruption that would continually work against his strident and sincere efforts at social reform and equity for those with the least. Though he was beloved by community members, particularly the poor who had benefited from his time as a doctor, and despite the fact that he was popular among voters, he may be best remembered for having achieved little, if any, lasting impact politically. This was mostly due to a hostile city council that thwarted Lane's best plans and forced him to veto their proposals time and again. The powerful business and saloon owners, not to mention those who operated houses of prostitution and speakeasies, maintained the *real* control over the financial and social agendas of the city. Lane was simply outnumbered.

The legacy Lane has left Oregon is not a paltry one. His contributions remain in the way he promoted health and nutrition programs for the poor, who were able to persevere because of that help, care and concern. His legacy remains in the work he did for women's rights in Portland, most notably the social services for prostitutes that he championed at a time when they were vilified rather than helped. He championed those "fallen women" who were often overlooked and ignored. These were women who became chronically ill due to venereal disease and the hidden agony of "pelvic inflammatory disease." PID was a common ailment of the time and caused women and young girls so much pain that they often sought relief with alcohol, opium and even heroin, often becoming drug addicts in the attempt to self-medicate. In addition, Lane appointed women to highly visible public offices that highlighted their skills and competence, helping increase employment opportunities for women.

One of Harry Lane's most significant appointments was that of Sarah Evans as market inspector. Sarah A. Evans was a Portland suffragist who exemplified the outspoken and aggressive tactics of the new generation in its fight to see women's rights expanded, promoted and accepted by society at large. She was a journalist and is best known for her tireless efforts to

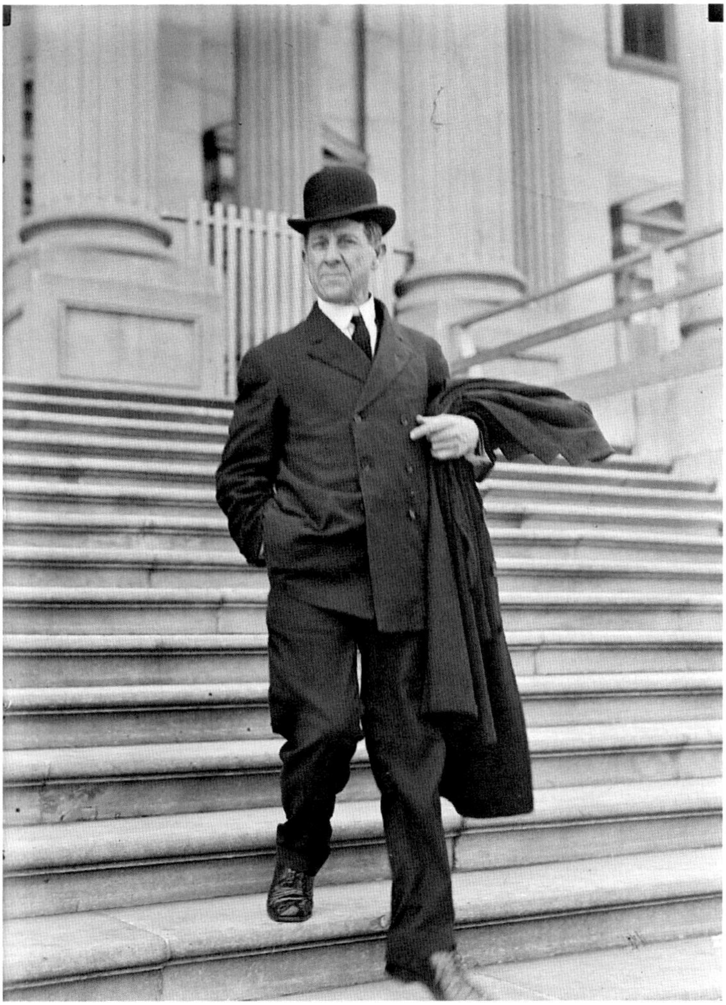

Dr. Harry Lane, Portland's beloved "people's doctor," was a popular mayor and Oregon's first popularly elected senator. Photo by Bain News Service. *U.S. Library of Congress.*

create and sustain free public libraries for the common citizens of Portland and for her support of education for women. As a lifelong activist, Evans was a member of the Portland Woman's Club, serving as its president in 1903 and 1904. She was also a member of the Young Women's Christian Association, the Oregon Equal Suffrage Association, the National Consumers League and the Portland Women's Union, along with the Oregon Federation of Women's Clubs, which she operated in 1905 and 1906.

In 1905, Evans became market inspector. Her job was to inspect the quality and cleanliness of local food stores to prevent local citizens from being poisoned by rotting meat and spoiled milk. Spoiled food was often sold at the turn of the century, with no regard for how it might impact the consumer. At a meeting in 1905, the city board of health, led by Evans's friend Dr. Esther Pohl Lovejoy, elected Evans to be the new Portland market inspector. Her appointment came with a recommendation from the School of Domestic Science. This was an important step but not the beginning of her crusade to protect Portlanders from dangerous food.

Evans was a charter member of the Portland Woman's Club and represented club women who were interested in "municipal housekeeping," which incorporated the domestic science movement of protecting the citizenry from poor-quality food. A dear friend and fellow suffragist of Evans, Esther Pohl Lovejoy, lost her seven-year-old son from drinking spoiled milk purchased at a local food market in Portland. The two women dedicated the rest of their lives to protecting the public. Evans took her position seriously, arising early to inspect markets and report her findings to not only the board of health but also the press. Her commitment clearly was to make certain there were no other deaths due to spoiled milk or rancid meat.

Evans became a formidable enemy to those who sold spoiled meat, vegetables and milk to unsuspecting Portlanders. Her inspections became the talk of the town, and sometimes there were conflicts. "The Excelsior Market on East Morrison and Union Avenue refused me admission. I was compelled to call a policeman. When I made the examination I found the place filthy," she reported. But she did find some improvement the year after her appointment when word had finally gotten through that markets had better comply with the new standards. Yet there were still those who resisted the changes the city wanted. She reported descriptions of coal tar–dyed shrimp, dyes in catsup and meat additives. On one occasion, she called the Humane Society to complain about a market's treatment of live chickens. Despite the improvements the markets agreed to make, there were still resisters. In September 1906, the owner of the Western Market "forcibly resisted" Evans's desire to take away a meat sample for later analysis. She then called Mayor Harry Lane, who gave her the authority of a special officer, with the power to arrest. Evans retired in 1935 at the age of eighty after working over thirty years as Portland's official market inspector, dying on a pension in 1940 at age eighty-five. She is one of the most notable examples of how a fierce spirit and a dedication to excellence altered Portland's landscape in a most positive manner.

Louise Bryant was the first female journalist to be hired by the *Oregonian*. Born in San Francisco, Bryant spent most of her formative years in Reno, Nevada, even attending the local university. As the daughter of the radical journalist Hugh Moran, she was raised to be an independent critical thinker, with progressive ideas and a desire to live life on her own terms.

When she learned she could transfer her college credits from Nevada State University to the University of Oregon, she moved to Eugene and joined the student body of fewer than five hundred. While at U of O, she became popular and sought after by both sexes. At a time when American culture was immersed in moralistic puritanism, particularly suffocating for women, Bryant rebelled against social restrictions and became the first woman on campus to openly wear "rouge" on her cheeks and mouth. She wrote for a small publication called *The Young Ladies Edition* and wrote a short story called "The Way of a Flirt" for a literary magazine called *Chuckwalla*. She contributed sketches to *Chuckwalla*, as well as to another literary review called *Artemisia*, and personified the independent spirit of a true bohemian.

Bryant is probably best remembered in Portland for the unique accomplishment of being the first female journalist hired by the *Oregonian*. This was a controversial change in the male-dominated newsroom where women's roles were minimal. Bryant's whole life was memorable, though, not only for her writing achievements but also for those people with whom she associated. After she graduated from the University of Oregon in 1909 with a degree in history, she moved from Eugene to Portland, where she pursued writing in its various genres, producing poetry, plays, society columns and human interest stories.

Bryant became firmly entrenched during this time in the Portland bohemian scene. Then, in late 1909, she met and married a handsome, blond dentist from a wealthy family named Paul Ahio Trullinger. They maintained their first of many homes on a houseboat on the Willamette River. During this time, she became close to Sara Bard Field, a leading feminist and poet. The whole time Bryant continued to write, contributing in 1912 to the radical journal *Blast*, a San Francisco weekly publication, edited by radical anarchist Alexander Berkman.

Though encouraged by her husband, Paul, who considered himself a free-thinking bohemian, and despite (or because of) having been published in various reviews and magazines, her marriage to Trullinger suffered. She detested housework and chafed under the domestic obligations of a married woman and a homemaker. After her marriage, she maintained her maiden name and even her previous downtown apartment in Portland, which probably only added to the stress in her marriage and may have further isolated her from "decent" society.

In 1915, Bryant's life took a sudden and unexpected turn when she met and fell in love with John Reed, a well-known Portland journalist and Harvard graduate. Reed focused his writing on labor issues, revolutions and various wars and had developed quite a following. During the Christmas holidays, he had come to Portland to spend time with his widowed mother and was introduced to Bryant at a dinner arranged by Helen Walters and other mutual friends. Bryant was instantly attracted to Reed, igniting an immediate love affair. Several days later, Walters wrote in her diary, "Jack has fallen in love with Louise and impetuously wants to take her to New York. We are endeavoring to avert scandal and save Paul." Reed hurried Bryant to Greenwich Village to be with him, and they were married in 1916.

Before their marriage, they lived openly together, in what Max Eastman, editor of *The Masses*, called "a gypsy compact." Reed encouraged Bryant's writing and got her in touch with influential writers and editors in New York. He later wrote to a friend, "I think I've found her at last. She's wild, brave and straight—and graceful and lovely to look at. In this spiritual vacuum, this unfertilized soil, she has grown (how I can't imagine) into an artist. She is coming to New York to get a job with me, I hope. I think she's the first person I ever loved without reservation."

Reed and Bryant were described as being ideal partners. They were both free spirits, disdainful of contemporary society and what the moral majority might think if they slept late or came home at odd hours, but their precociousness and impulsive natures were also a detriment to reason and decision making, and they both suffered from spur of the moment ideas and schemes. The marriage to Reed didn't last long. After only four years together, Reed died on October 19, 1920. By then, Bryant was a recognized and respected journalist in her own right. Partly because of Reed's influence and partly because of her own commitment to social justice, Bryant became a committed socialist and spent the rest of her life advocating for peace and justice around the world.

As a reporter for the *Oregonian*, Bryant chafed at the "puff pieces" and "human interest" stories she was routinely assigned, preferring to write about the achievements and hardships of women's lives. In 1912, she did a series of stories on women with unique achievements, highlighting, among others, the careers of Mary Frances Isom and Lola Baldwin. Her in-depth look at the Women's Protective Division is an important source of information on the dangers Portland presented for young women. Using false names,

Bryant tells the stories of several young women who were lured to the city by unscrupulous men who exploited and then discarded them. These stories give a human face to the "vice district" that preyed on vulnerable young women, exposing them to venereal disease and risking their lives with drug addiction and illegal, unsafe abortions.

Abortions had been illegal, but available, in Portland since 1870. The law was rarely enforced and usually came up only when the mother died during the operation. With the procedure illegal, most doctors refused to

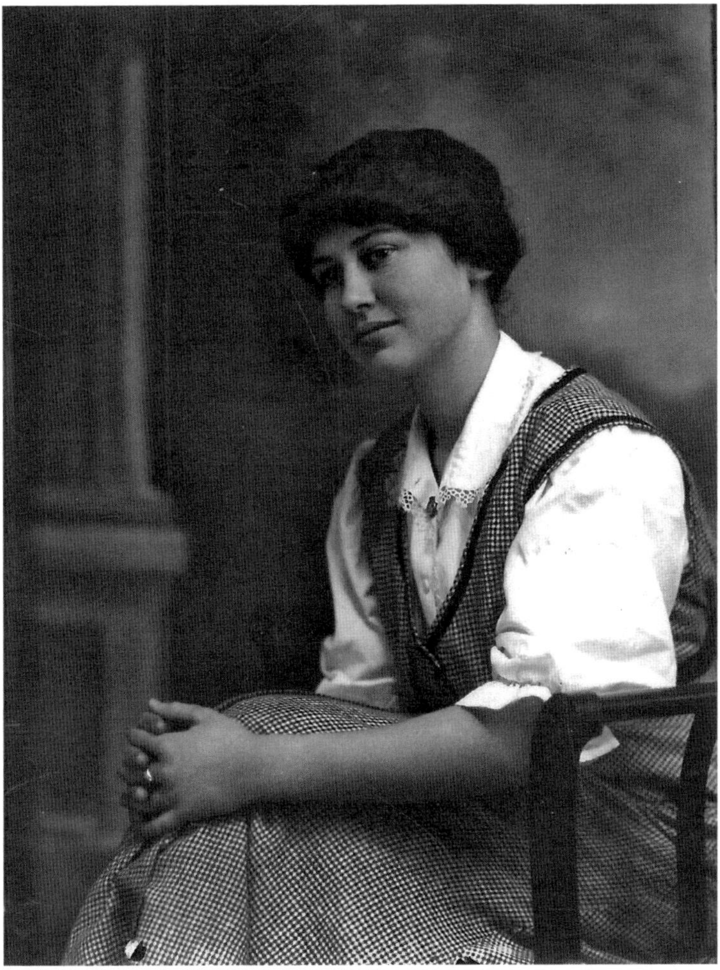

Anna Schrader came to Portland in 1910, escaping a bad marriage in her native Minnesota. She found success and adventure in Portland until her life was ruined by scandal in 1929. Photograph by Tom Cronise. *Oregon State Library.*

perform it, and women were forced to go to poorly trained or disbarred doctors and charlatans. In 1908 alone, three women died during abortions: Pearl Lamb, Stella Bennett and Bessie Crippin. Each case resulted in a manslaughter charge against the doctor and a humiliating public trial. Dr. Marie Equi and Dr. Alys Griff, both specialists in women's health, recognized the need for safe abortions and offered the service to their patients. Dr. Griff was much better at discretion than Equi so little is known about her practice. Dr. Equi, who had friends and connections in all classes of Portlanders from the high to the low, was a passionate and committed woman who provided her patients with abortions or layettes as necessary—a tradition that was carried on into the next generation by Dr. Ruth Barnett. Equi protected herself by providing abortions to women who needed them whether they came from a brothel or a wealthy family and being willing to blackmail any city official who might try to bring charges against her. That kind of assertive attitude has always been respected in Portland.

Anna Schrader was another of the women who came to Portland during the Girl Rush, arriving in 1910. Census records indicate she was married at the age of eighteen, presumably in Minnesota, where she was born and raised. She became a gadfly for the local Portland police and provided them with a great deal of useful information regarding bootlegging during prohibition. This was all possible because of her affair with police lieutenant William Breuning, who had gotten her the job of "private detective." When the affair started in 1921, both were married to other people, and they were able to keep it secret from their spouses. She became an important member of the mayor's secret police and provided evidence for a number of arrests for violating liquor laws. Although never an official member of the police bureau, Schrader received extensive police training and was accepted and trusted by many officers. When her sexual relationship with Breuning soured in the late '20s, he attempted to discard her, but Schrader showed her tenacity and the importance of the information she had been collecting. The resulting scandal shook the police bureau, if not the city.

# CHAPTER 3
# OUR GEORGE

*The time has come and is now here: When every good citizen's conduct, if not his conscience, must come into accord with the wishes and designs of the United States government.*
*–Judge George Rossman*

February 19, 1917, was cold and rainy in Portland. That's why four Internal Revenue Service (IRS) agents were in their office at the U.S. Customs House that afternoon. The four men—Miles, Smith, McGill and Littell—spent the afternoon looking out the window at the Golden West Hotel just across the street. By 1917, the Golden West had become the largest African American–owned business in town and the center of the black community in Portland. The police also suspected that it was the distribution center for one of the largest bootlegging rings in the city. Multnomah County sheriff's deputy George Hardin, Portland's first black police officer, had spent months on surveillance and infiltration of the hotel but had only been able to make a few low-level arrests of Pullman porters for possession of liquor. As the four IRS agents watched, a large touring car, driven by a white man, stopped in front of the hotel. They perked up, hoping this might be the evidence they needed to help the police shut down bootlegging at the Golden West.

The touring car was painted with a sign advertising the Advance Auto Touring Company and driven by Charles Meins, a local chauffeur. Meins parked the car in front of the hotel's entrance, and O.D. Thomas jumped

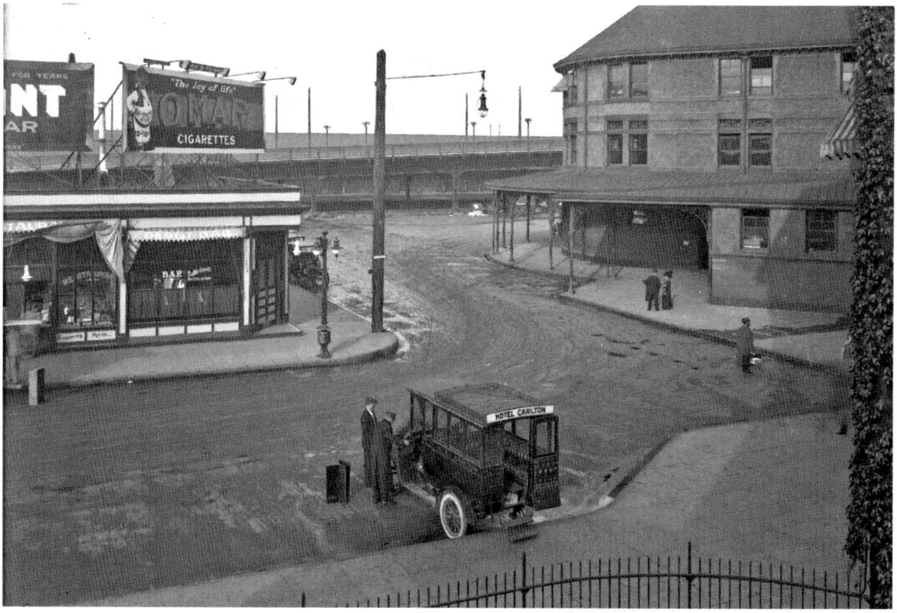


Union Depot was the most reliable source of illegal liquor in Portland during prohibition. The Pullman porters ring was very inventive in its technique and efficient at bribing police officers. *Portland City Archive.*

out and hustled two large suitcases in through the front door. The four IRS agents claimed that they had not been conducting surveillance against the hotel but had just happened to glance out the window. Their actions show that they knew what they were looking at. One of the agents called Central Precinct and summoned Detective Charles B. Hill, telling him that a liquor deal was in progress at the Golden West Hotel. One IRS agent stayed at the window, and the three others went down to the street to keep a closer eye on Meins and Thomas. Detective Hill covered the few blocks from Central Precinct to the Golden West in minutes, and as he and the IRS agents watched, a black man, who was never identified, came out of the hotel with one of Thomas's suitcases and handed it to him. The black man went back into the hotel, and Thomas took the suitcase, now noticeably heavier, to the car. Hill arrested him and inside the suitcase found twelve quart bottles of whiskey wrapped in blankets and packed with straw. The detective also took Meins into custody and called for a paddy wagon. As Hill was handcuffing the two men, the black man came out of the hotel with the other suitcase. Seeing the police activity on the street, he dropped the suitcase and ran back into the hotel. Hill chased him, but the unidentified black man got away.

Back at Central Precinct, deputy district attorney Richard Deich interrogated Thomas and Meins and then told Captain Chester Innskeep that they had enough evidence to raid the hotel. Innskeep dispatched Lieutenant Leon Jenkins with a dozen patrolmen and detectives to raid the building. Within a few minutes, three large cars pulled up in front of the Golden West Hotel, and policemen were assigned to cover every door. Jenkins placed Al Green, the manager on duty, under arrest and proceeded to the fifth floor to begin a top-down, room-by-room search for illegal liquor.

The fifth floor had been added to the building only a few years before and provided the most up-to-date and luxurious suites in the hotel. In the meantime, the top floor of the Golden West had become one of the most prestigious addresses for a black man in Portland. The suites on that floor were occupied by men who made more money than could be predicted by the jobs they held—mostly porters, chauffeurs and bootblacks. Within minutes, it would be clear how they made at least some of their money. The first cache of liquor Lieutenant Jenkins and his men found was in the room of P.L. Broy on the fifth floor. The bottles matched the ones in Thomas's suitcase, but Broy insisted that someone else had left them in his room. The police confiscated several quarts of whiskey from Broy's room, but for some reason they didn't arrest him. Broy disappears from our story at this point, so he may have left town.

The next cache of liquor was also found on the fifth floor, in the room of Dave Thornton. Thornton was a Pullman porter on the Southern Pacific Railroad who would die in a questionable suicide two years later in an auto wrecking garage on Northwest Broadway, just a few blocks from the hotel. There is some reason to believe that the Auto Wrecking Co. Inc., which occupied the building where Thornton died, was being used by car thieves to strip down stolen cars. Auto theft was the fastest-growing crime in Portland in 1917, and in 1920 the police bureau would create an Auto Theft Bureau to try and deal with the problem. Dave Thornton would be found in the garage with a bullet in his brain in 1919. During the 1917 Golden West Hotel raid, police found a cask of sherry, five quarts of gin and two of whiskey in Thornton's room, along with trays, glasses and ice. It is likely that Thornton was running a speakeasy in his suite.

Al Green, the manager on duty at the hotel and the proprietor of the candy store that had replaced the now illegal saloon at the Golden West, had eight bottles of bonded whiskey in his room, but it was in John Lowe's room that Lieutenant Jenkins made his biggest haul. The police didn't know it yet, but Lowe was one of the leaders of the Pullman porter bootlegging ring.

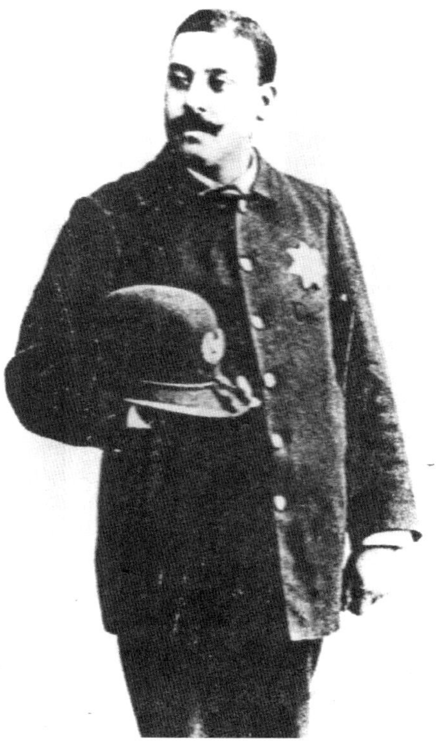

George Hardin was a Portland police officer in the 1890s and then worked for years as a bartender and teamster before becoming Multnomah County's first black sheriff's deputy. He was well suited for undercover work at the Golden West Hotel and was zealous at hunting down bootleggers. *Portland Police Historical Society.*

Rivalry over leadership would eventually push Lowe out, and he would take his revenge violently while increasing his power and influence with the police. In the 1917 raid, the police found twenty-two quarts of whiskey in his room and hauled him in.

The February 1917 raid at the Golden West was not the first, or the last, the hotel would suffer. Prostitution and gambling had been fixtures at the hotel since William Allen and his silent partner, Al Wohlers, took over the place in 1906. Wohlers, an ex-policeman, saloonkeeper and pimp, was one of the most powerful "fixers" in the North End, and rumor had it that he was the payoff bagman for the city government and the police bureau. After a series of prostitution raids at the Golden West in 1907, Wohlers had negotiated a settlement with the city, and the hotel had been left alone for nearly a decade. During that time, the Golden West had solidified its place in Portland's African American community, and the aging Wohlers had increased his power and influence. It was not enough to keep the police away when the Pullman porter bootlegging ring began to operate out of the Golden West in 1916, though.

After the first year of prohibition enforcement, it was clear that the law was a failure. As Mayor H. Russell Albee told a Woman's Christian Temperance Union (WCTU) audience in the spring of 1916, the liquor men were making as much money as they had before Oregon went dry. The truth was that they were probably making more money than they had. The price of liquor had soared to $7 per quart, a previously unheard-of price, and with no liquor license fees to pay, the saloon men were raking it in. While the prohibition law was beneficial to liquor sellers, the city suffered. The *Oregonian* estimated that Portland lost over $300,000 per year in liquor license revenues, and the steady flow of bootlegging fines (between $25 and $100) was hardly enough to cover the increased court and police costs.

Mayor Albee was in a serious bind: with depleted revenues he was challenged to keep the city running, but he didn't have the political support to raise taxes. The WCTU was mostly in denial about the liquor business that continued, but the Anti-Saloon League and the Law and Order League kept up pressure for increased enforcement. Several publicity-seeking Protestant pastors helped keep pressure on the city as well. Episcopal bishop Walter Sumner set the tone when he denounced Portland's North End as a blot on the city to a national bishops' conference in 1916. Soon, ambitious pastors, mostly from the east side, began visiting the North End in disguise and then describing the shocking conditions they found there to their congregations. This tactic was highly embarrassing to the city government and usually resulted in increased raids—no matter how ineffectual they were.

The police raids were unsuccessful for many reasons. First, they were usually made at the lowest levels, arresting bartenders, delivery men and individual drinkers. These arrests did nothing to stem the flow of liquor and resulted in small fines or, at most, a few days in jail. Second, the laws were confusing. For example, possession of liquor was not illegal, but making, selling or transporting it was. Requirements for search warrants were debatable, and several times the police were forced to return seized liquor and drop charges. Third, juries were reluctant to convict people for liquor offenses, especially when the evidence disappeared. And the evidence did disappear. There were several cases of liquor evidence disappearing out of Central Precinct or the Multnomah County Courthouse. There were at least two cases in Portland where juries drank the evidence during deliberations and then acquitted the accused bootleggers for lack of evidence. Portland's first year of trying to enforce the prohibition law did not bode well for national Prohibition.

The February 1917 raid on the Golden West Hotel was an attempt to show that Portland was serious about enforcing the law. As propaganda, it was successful; as law enforcement, it was a failure. Charles Mien and O.D. Thomas were acquitted of liquor charges, and none of the other suspects was charged. The flow of booze from the Southern Pacific Railroad was not even slowed. The sheriff's department and the police bureau were not through with the Golden West Hotel or the Pullman porter bootlegging ring,

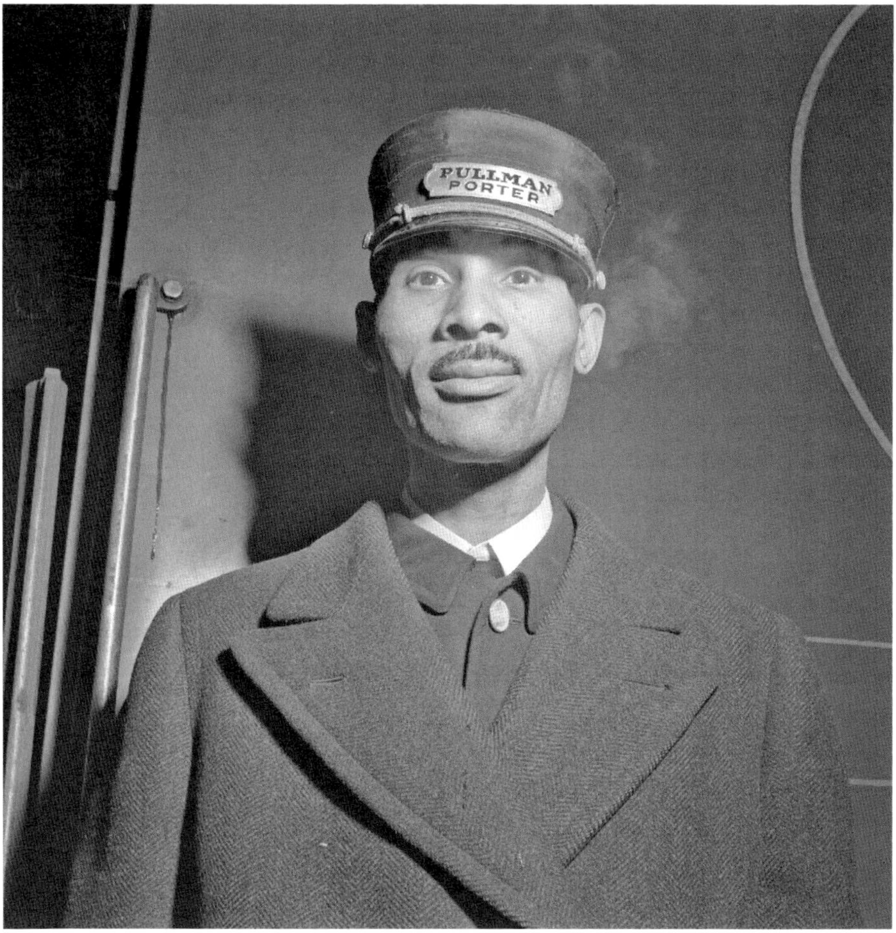


For the first half of the twentieth century, Pullman porter was the most prestigious job that an African American man could aspire to. Pullman porters, secretly organized by A. Phillip Randolph as the Brotherhood of Sleeping Car Porters, played a vital role in developing and spreading African American culture. Photograph by Jack Delano. *U.S. Library of Congress.*

though. Conflict between these parties would exist until 1920 or 1921, when Tom Johnson got control of the bootleg ring and made peace with the city. Whiskey, first illegal and later un-taxed, continued to flow into Portland via the Southern Pacific well into the 1950s.

The Golden West raid and the battle with the Pullman porters' ring set the pattern for prohibition enforcement in Portland: with the priority being enforcement of the dry laws against minorities and immigrants. The protection of fixers, such as Al Wohlers, insulated the managers, like W.D.

Allen and Al Green, from serious trouble. Lower-level operators, like Dave Thornton, had much more to fear from one another than from the police.

Watching from the wings was Mayor Albee's successor, city commissioner George Luis Baker, who would be elected mayor in June 1917, just six weeks after U.S. entry into the Great War. Baker, who had served on the city council off and on since the 1890s, had been preparing his run for mayor since his last election victory in 1915. Baker was a large, jovial man who had been one of the city's most popular actors after his arrival in Portland around 1890. Born in the Dalles to a poor family, Baker spent much of his childhood traveling from town to town, following his father, who was a transient worker. Before the age of ten, Baker dropped out of school to help support his family by selling newspapers on the streets of San Francisco. As he always liked to say, George Baker was a self-made man.

Baker embodied many of the qualities immortalized, and satirized, in Sinclair Lewis's 1920 novel *Babbit.* He idolized "manliness": two-fisted, hard-drinking and a lover of "blood sport." When he took on a job, he approached it with "pep" and enthusiasm. When he faced an issue, his goal was to "punch it square on the nose." Like many of his generation, he felt ethics were for show, and his noble ends sometimes justified the dirtiest means. Gregarious and jovial, Baker was immensely popular as both a theater manager and as a politician. His campaign literature listed nearly twenty organizations he was a member of: the Elks, Moose, Rotarians, Masons and others. He was a joiner who never met a fraternal or social organization he didn't like. One of the most interesting groups he joined was the Ex-Newsboys' Association (ENA), made up of men who had sold papers on the streets as boys. The ENA included several members who would become rich and powerful during the Baker administration, such as Eddie Tonkin and J.J. Parker. It also included a good percentage of men involved with organized crime, such as Augustine Ardiss (aka Bobby Evans), I.G. Ankelis and Paul Ails. The younger generation of the ENA included Terry Schrunk, the only Portland mayor besides George Baker himself to serve four terms.

By 1903, Baker had moved from acting into theater management. He owned the Baker Theater in Portland, as well as the Baker City Opera House, and he organized the Baker Stock Company Players, which became the most popular theater company in the state as it traveled from town to town presenting theatrical pieces. In Portland, Baker endeared himself by enthusiastically boosting public projects, tirelessly working as city commissioner and organizing wild parties for visiting conventioneers and a group of cronies made up of some of the most powerful merchants in town, as well as ambitious young men he knew from the Ex-Newsboys' Association. Baker's parties took one of two forms: *smokers*, small, intimate gatherings that usually included boxing matches, as well as heavy drinking and smoking, or *antics* (also known as Jinks or High Jinks). Antics were huge parties, sometimes held at the Portland Hotel, for visiting conventioneers. Antics often had more than one hundred guests and included gambling, drinking and entertainment. Baker had a succession of beautiful young actresses who served as his protégés. These women were often the stars of Baker's antics and were supported by an attractive chorus line in scanty (for the times) costumes.

One of the most notorious of Baker's antics occurred just a few weeks after he took office as mayor in 1918, when the Oregon Auto Dealers held its annual convention at the Multnomah Hotel in Portland. Baker was an avid car enthusiast who had owned cars since at least 1903, and he outdid himself for the car dealers' convention. The party got so wild that the police staged a rare raid at the Multnomah Hotel because of public complaints. No one was arrested for drinking; presumably, the police looked the other way, but one of the performers, Blanche Ford, was arrested for "indecent dancing."

Weeks before his election as mayor, George Baker must have noted the raid at the Golden West Hotel with interest. Already making plans for his own administration, Baker had two clear priorities where prohibition was concerned: to present a good front and create a good reputation for enforcement of the law and to keep liquor available for himself and his friends. There is no "smoking gun" evidence to prove that Baker colluded with bootleggers, but the proof is in the results. By 1922, Portland had the reputation for the best enforcement of prohibition in the country, and the price of a quart of whiskey had shot up to fifteen dollars, one of the highest prices in the country. At the same time, the North End continued to operate "wide open," speakeasies and stills flourished on the east side and uniformed police officers made regular deliveries of liquor to city hall from the evidence room in Central Precinct. Portland police officer Floyd Marsh noted in his autobiography, *Twenty Years a Soldier of Fortune* (1976), that in addition to all this, Portland became the central distribution point for bonded whiskey on the West Coast during this time. Somehow George Baker managed to have his booze and drink it, too.

In addition to prohibition, Baker had two other issues on his mind as he prepared for the election. First was the war that was raging in Europe between Germany and Austria on one side and Great Britain, France and Russia on the other. In 1917, the war had been going on for three years and had already left several million dead and the combatants on the verge of economic collapse. President Woodrow Wilson, who was reelected in 1916 with the slogan "He kept us out of war," was finding it more and more difficult to keep that promise. Facing unrestricted warfare by German submarines in the Atlantic, in February 1917, Congress was debating the arming of U.S. merchant ships for self-defense. After the loss of several American vessels, Wilson would ask Congress for a declaration of war against Germany in April. Baker, a very patriotic man who loved a good show, was ready to do more than his share for the war effort.

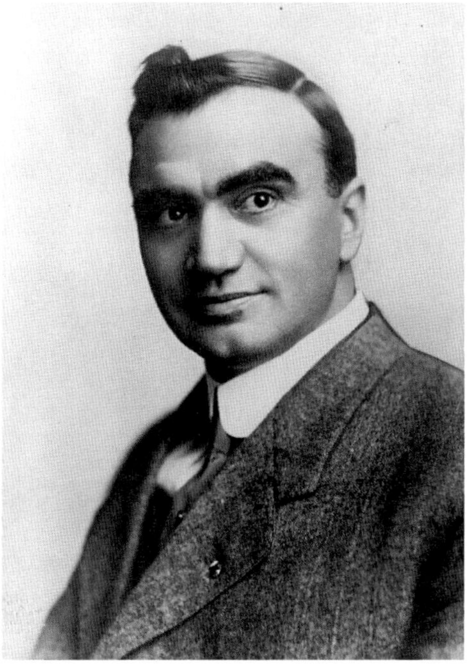

George Luis Baker served as Portland mayor from 1918 to 1933. He embodied many of the attributes and attitudes satirized by Sinclair Lewis in his 1920 novel *Babbit*. A one-man chamber of commerce, Baker was beloved by many Portlanders and affectionately called "Our George." *Oregon Historical Society.*

The second issue on Baker's mind was the growing strength of radical labor organizers. Ever since the Portland Free Speech Fight in 1913, in conjunction with the Oregon Packing Co. Cannery strike, the Industrial Workers of the World (IWW), known as the Wobblies, had been building strength by organizing workers in the logging camps of Oregon and Washington, as well as sawmill, cannery and unemployed workers in the cities of the Northwest. Although Mayor Albee used violent repression, infiltration and even attempts to frame Wobblies organizers for murder, nothing he did could stop their growing power. Ironically, Albee came under intense pressure and lost much of his political support for being "soft on the IWW." George Baker was determined that charge would never be raised against him, and he was already making plans to suppress the Wobblies and destroy them once and for all, if he could.

Under the commission charter, passed in 1913 with enthusiastic support from city councilman Baker, mayoral elections were nonpartisan, but party support was apparent in the 1917 election. Baker was a registered Republican with the full support of Multnomah County's strong Republican Party. Will H. Daly, his strongest rival, was also a Republican, but he drew strong support from a coalition of Democratic and Progressive Party activists. Baker was vocally pro-union and always willing to pander to the labor vote, but his labor support couldn't help him against Daly, a true union activist. Daly had served as head of the Oregon Labor Federation, a member of the Portland Central Labor Council and an official of the Typographical Union. Daly, a linotype operator for the *Oregonian* until 1911, was the owner-operator of a print shop in southeast Portland. He was the most visible member of a unique coalition of union members and small business owners described by historian Robert Johnston in his book *The Radical Middle Class* (2003). With the IWW pulling the Portland labor movement to the left, activists from the Progressive Party and Daly's coalition were able to build real power closer to the center. Daly, who introduced IWW leader Bill Haywood at a 1909 rally, was a popular political candidate. He served on the city council from 1911 to 1917 and went into the June 1917 election as the clear front-runner for mayor.

Daly, like any good union official, had strong enemies, including Henry Pittock of the *Oregonian* and Franklin T. Griffith of Portland Railway, Power and Light. Both Pittock and Griffith were close friends and strong supporters of George Baker. Griffith's opposition to Daly was political; Daly supported "jitneys," an early form of independent taxis that threatened the monopoly of Griffith's streetcars. Pittock's animosity toward his ex-employee was more personal; as utility commissioner, Daly had forced the installation of water meters for all Bull Run water customers and exposed a corrupt deal between Pittock and the city to provide a pipeline of water at city expense to Pittock's hilltop mansion, more than a mile outside the city limits. Historian Shawn Daley points at Pittock's personal animosity toward Daly for the *Oregonian*'s dirty tricks in the 1917 election, but it was probably compounded by Pittock's fear of a mayor who would really promote the interests of working people. Whatever the motivation, Pittock's newspaper took drastic action against Daly's campaign and doomed his election.

On June 2, 1917, three days before the election, Daly's southeast Portland home was burglarized. Valuables were ignored, but Daly's files were thoroughly searched. The only thing the burglars took was an uncompleted application for Socialist Party membership dated 1910. With U.S. entry into the Great War in April, the country was being swept by a wave of ultra-patriotism. Stimulated by effective propaganda campaigns by both the U.S. and the British governments, much of the nation's anger was aimed at the pacifist Socialist Party. On June 3, Pittock ran an editorial, disguised as a news story, on the front page of the *Morning Oregonian*, under the headline "Security of City Hangs on Election." In the editorial, Pittock implied that Daly was a "labor agitator" and "walking boss for the IWW." He also bluntly stated that Portland's blossoming shipbuilding industry, so vital to the war effort, would be endangered if Daly became mayor. The next day, the *Oregonian* ran an ad claiming that Daly had participated in plans by the Central Labor Council to shut down both the steel industry and the shipbuilding industry in Portland. The ad didn't mention that the plans were made during a strike that had ended months before. There was also a sly mention in a story about a baseball game of "Daly taking out a Socialist card." In the same issue, Pittock ran a copy of the stolen Socialist Party application under the headline "Daly Socialist Since 1910." Daly's supporters couldn't have been surprised by the *Oregonian*'s smear campaign, or Daly's sympathy for socialist ideas, but the tactic was enough to let Baker squeak into office by a small margin.

Historian Shawn Daley states that Pittock approved the burglary and that it was carried out by members of the *Oregonian* staff. Maybe that's true, but the tactic was used by George Baker in later elections as well. Most notorious was the 1932 recall election, when the mayor's good friend and payoff master, Bobby Evans, coordinated the burglary of campaign headquarters and theft of a good number of petitions in a partly successful effort to stop the election. Former police officer Floyd Marsh stated that as head of the "mayor's secret police" he had people he could call on for "anything short of murder." It is very possible that Baker learned this technique from his friend Henry Pittock.

Elected in June 1917, Baker didn't take office until January 1918. In the meantime, his priority was the war effort. As mayor-elect, Baker began his practice of seeing off the men leaving for military service; soon, he was holding "going-away" breakfasts for hundreds of doughboys at a time at the Civic Auditorium. "God bless you, boys," was the mayor-elect's famous slogan. Baker also took the lead in raising money for the war effort by selling War Savings Stamps and Liberty Bonds. There were two national War Stamp drives before Baker took office, and Portland exceeded its quota both times, partly through Baker's efforts.

The third war drive, in the spring of 1918, prompted Julius Meier, a Republican Party activist and head of the Meier and Frank Department Store, to suggest the building of a Liberty Temple in the middle of Fifth Avenue, between the Portland Hotel and the Pioneer Courthouse. The building, erected in one day under George Baker's supervision and flanked

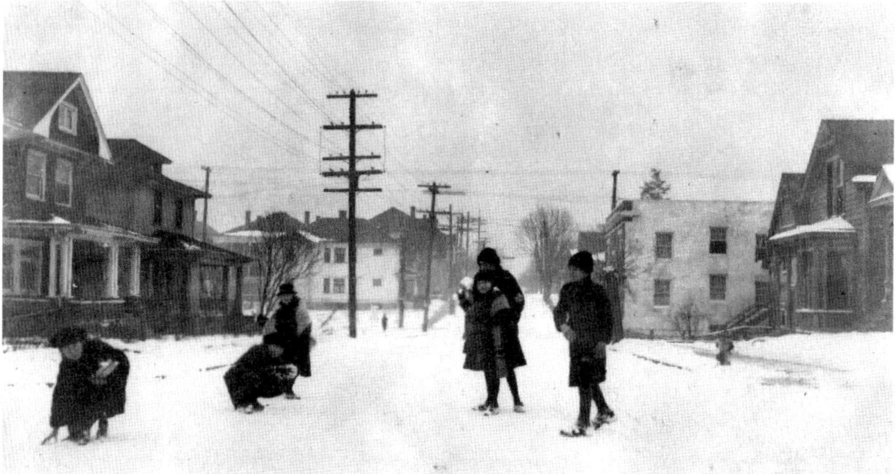

No matter how big a city Portland becomes, it always has the feel of a small town. This is never more true than the rare times that it snows. *Portland City Archive.*

by two replicas of the Statue of Liberty, became the center of fundraising for the war effort and the site of many rousing patriotic and xenophobic speeches. Rumors of financial irregularity surrounded the Liberty Temple project, as they did all of the construction projects that Julius Meier and George Baker were involved in. According to historian E. Kimbark MacColl, there is no evidence that Baker ever personally profited from the corruption in his administration, but many of his friends did.

The nation had been wary of Germans since the explosion of the Black Tom Armory in New Jersey and the bombing campaign against allied ships in New York Harbor during the summer of 1916. The fact that a German sabotage ring had been caught operating in New York was added to outrageous stories of German atrocities in Belgium and France by the sophisticated propaganda apparatus set up by the U.S. and British governments. The result was a harsh anti-German campaign that swept the nation. In Portland, individuals and mobs harassed and beat anyone with a German, or German-sounding, name or language. With one of four Portlanders born outside the United States and indiscriminate, xenophobic mobs who couldn't tell the difference between German, Dutch, Yiddish or even Russian, there were many targets. Restaurateurs abolished the offensive-sounding "hamburger"; the popular sandwich became known as the Liberty Steak. In the southeast Brooklyn neighborhood, the names of three streets that sounded German were changed to the names of allied generals.

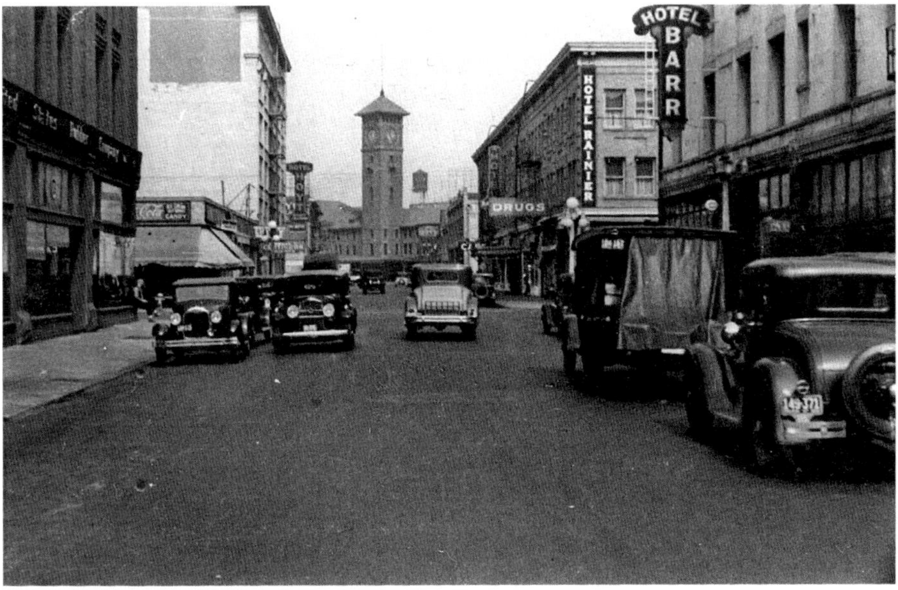


The area between Burnside Street and the Union Depot, known as "Coontown" to the police bureau, was home to the majority of black Portlanders in the early decades of the twentieth century. *Portland City Archive.*

Anti-German hysteria swept the city. With the passage of the Espionage Act (1917), which made it illegal to interfere with military preparation or discourage anyone from enlisting, and the Sedition Act (1918), which criminalized criticism of the government, that hysteria had legal teeth. The Sedition Act was repealed in 1919, but the Espionage Act is still in force. During the Great War, both laws were used to jail hundreds of people for deeds that would not normally be crimes. Dr. Marie Equi was sentenced to three years in San Quentin for speaking against the war at a rally. Louise Olivereau, an anarchist, poet and teacher at the Portland Modern School, served two years for speaking against the war. The most absurd case was that of Henry Albers, the owner of one of Portland's most visible and prosperous flour mills. Albers, born in Germany, got drunk on the Southern Pacific Railroad (thanks to the Pullman porters) while returning from a business trip. He was overheard singing songs in German and charged with sedition. Albers was convicted and sentenced to three years in prison. He died of a stroke in July 1921 in the middle of a long appeals process. Stress from negative publicity and ostracism by his neighbors is credited for his death. Even Harry Lane, the "people's doctor," popular Portland ex-mayor and U.S. senator was not immune. One of six senators to vote against U.S. entry into the war, Lane was vilified in the papers and roundly denounced by people he thought were his friends. He died of a stroke while returning to Portland to face the criticism; again, stress was a contributing cause to his death.

Even passive resistance to the war could be severely punished as M. Louise Hunt found out. Hunt, born in Portland, Maine, in 1876, came to Portland by way of Philadelphia's Drexel Institute and the Lansing, Michigan public library. She was hired as an assistant by Mary Frances Isom, the founding librarian of the Portland Library Association (PLA). Oregon had an advanced library system—the finest in the West, according to historian Stewart Holbrook—which had just finished a decade of incredible growth. By 1917, most communities in the state were served by public libraries or the portable libraries that served remote rural communities. The Portland Central Library on Southwest Tenth Avenue was the jewel in the crown of the Oregon library system.

When war broke out, the state's librarians saw a chance to prove their usefulness in a national emergency and to increase their membership. The public libraries served several purposes during the war: they became vital sources of information and war news; they worked closely with the Red Cross to provide emergency training for civilians and reading material for army bases and hospitals; they censored books considered pro-German or that "promoted pacifism"; and they participated in fundraising by selling War Savings Stamps and Liberty Bonds. Louise Hunt was assigned to staff a War Stamp kiosk in the lobby of the Central Library.

By all accounts, Louise Hunt was a good employee who did her job diligently. Her problem was that she was a pacifist at a time when the pastor of her Methodist church was quoted as saying, "There is no place on this side of American soil for a pacifist." Before the war, Hunt made a trip to Washington, D.C., to lobby Oregon's congressional delegation to keep America out of the war. She was met with hostility by all except Senator Lane. After the war began, she kept quiet about her feelings. She diligently sold War Savings Stamps, but she refused to buy any herself.

In April 1917, the PLA board received an anonymous letter accusing Hunt of disloyalty and complaining about the fact that she had not bought any War Stamps or Liberty Bonds. The board investigated the charges, and after Mary Isom testified to Hunt's loyalty and diligence as an employee, they cleared her of wrongdoing. Board member W.F. Woodward, a rabid "super-patriot" who had tried to burn such "pro-German" books as the works of Johann Goethe and poet Heinrich Heine, was not satisfied with the board's verdict and leaked the anonymous letter to the press. The scandal was huge.

After several days of strident press coverage and a denunciation from Mayor Baker, who said that Hunt's attitude was an "insult to the motherhood of our nation," Louise Hunt resigned her position and returned to her family home in Maine.

The Industrial Workers of the World (IWW) came under attack for disloyalty as well. Since its founding in 1905, the IWW had found its greatest success in the logging camps and lumber mills of the Pacific Northwest. The logging operators who employed the vast number of lumber workers in Oregon and Washington were extremely individualistic; one of the few things they could agree on was opposition to collective bargaining with their employees. They particularly didn't like dealing with the radical IWW, but they wouldn't bargain fairly with the more conservative American Federation of Labor Timber Workers Union either. The intransigence of the employers forced the workers to become more confrontational, and by the early summer of 1917 several small "wildcat" strikes were developing into a big strike that could paralyze the lumber industry.

The wildcat strikes began over unsafe working and unhealthy living conditions in the logging camps, but as the IWW took over leadership, they added demands for an eight-hour day and a closed shop—in which all employees would be union members. Increased demands made the employers even more intransigent, and lumber production dropped to a small fraction of what it had been. Although Washington's governor supported the strikers' demand for an eight-hour day, he ordered the mass arrest of strikers who were held in internment camps all over the state. IWW organizers were separated from the other workers, and many of them were tried under the Espionage Act and imprisoned or deported. Becoming more desperate, the IWW leadership in Spokane called for a general strike in which all industries would be shut down in sympathy with the "political prisoners." The general strike call led to martial law in Spokane and even more arrests. By the end of the summer, most of the Wobbly leadership was in jail, and the remaining loggers decided to "take the strike to the job." Returning to work, they worked so slowly and inefficiently that lumber production dropped even further.

The U.S. War Department watched the developing situation worriedly. Lumber was a vital resource for the war effort, used for building railroad cars, ships and airplanes. The War Department estimated that the military needed ten million board feet of lumber every month; the troubled logging industry was barely producing two million. In response, the U.S. Army created the Spruce Division and sent soldiers into the woods to break the strike once and for all. Many of the imprisoned strikers were drafted and forced to go back to work as soldiers. Floyd Marsh, a young man from Arizona, served as a medical orderly for the Spruce Division during the war and was stationed at Vancouver, Washington, and Waldport, Oregon. It was his first look at Portland, where he settled in 1923 and later joined the police bureau.

In November 1917, the War Department created the Loyal Legion of Loggers and Lumbermen (Four L), which functioned as a "company union" with no right to strike. The Four L, backed up by military authority and thousands of soldiers, forced the employers to accept the eight-hour day and to improve living conditions and worker safety. Before the end of 1918, the Pacific Northwest was producing over twenty million board feet of lumber every month. Most of the IWW leadership was dead, in prison or had been deported, and the union's power in the Pacific Northwest was broken. Wobblies began to hide their allegiance to industrial organizing. Many of them drifted into other occupations and joined the unions they found there. In Portland, the main Wobbly influence was seen in the International Longshoremen's Association, the Sailors' Union of the Pacific and other waterfront unions.

## CHAPTER 4

# THE GREATEST NEED OF THE DAY

*I'm not a match in talking to a high class socialist.*
*—George L. Baker*

As the war ground to a close in the fall of 1918, the world was faced with an even deadlier problem. The war's disruption of normal life and the massive worldwide movement of troops created the perfect conditions for the influenza virus. The Spanish flu pandemic of 1918–20 infected hundreds of millions of people around the world and killed between 50 and 100 million people, creating one of the world's most deadly health crises.

The first sign of the flu in Portland appeared on October 3, 1918, when Private James McNeese, a soldier in transit from Camp Lewis, came into the county hospital with a high fever. Influenza had already reached epidemic levels in Boston and other eastern cities, so McNeese was isolated and transferred to the military hospital at Fort Vancouver. Within a couple of days, there were more than thirty cases of flu in a military training detachment at Benson High School. Benson was immediately quarantined and transformed into the city's first makeshift emergency hospital. By the end of the month, more than one thousand Portlanders had the flu, and the Civic Auditorium had been transformed into an emergency hospital as well. The public schools were closed and public gatherings restricted.

Rumors of the war's end were finally realized on November 11, but there were few celebrations as the restriction on public gatherings was still in place. Worried about business as the Christmas shopping season began and swayed by citizens who said it was nothing more than a bad cold bug, Mayor Baker unilaterally repealed the public gathering ban and reopened the schools on November 16.

Two weeks later, when the emergency hospital at Civic Auditorium was scheduled to close, flu cases were on the rise again and the hospital was left open. On December 11, the city imposed a strict quarantine on anyone with flu-like symptoms and their family members. The quarantine was highly unpopular, and many people evaded it, spreading the flu even more. By January 4, 1919, there were more than 200 new flu cases being reported each day. Between January 12 and 19, there were more than 1,800 new flu cases reported. Many people started wearing protective masks over their faces, and panic was beginning to set in.

Over the next week, flu cases tapered off, and by January 31, 1919, the City Health Commission reported that the epidemic in Portland was over, although cases of flu continued for several more months. More than 3,600 Oregonians died of influenza, almost three times as many as were lost in the Great War.

In October 1918, right at the start of the flu epidemic in Oregon, the state bar association met for its annual convention. The lawyers assembled to discuss the need for new laws after the war. Prosecutors especially liked the Sedition Act, which could be used selectively to target radical groups like the IWW. The bar association, recognizing that the war was nearing its end and that the Sedition Act would end with it, called for a criminal syndicalism law. Idaho and California had already passed laws making it a felony to join radical groups like the IWW. Many members of the state's establishment felt Oregon needed such a law as well.

Events in Portland added urgency to the call for a criminal syndicalism law. Repression of the IWW led many on the left to try and build large coalitions of workers, demobilized soldiers and the unemployed. Portland's shipbuilding industry had been stimulated by the war and attracted thousands of new workers to the city, swelling the population. Canceled contracts after the war ended led to severe unemployment. By January 1919, Portland had more than ten thousand unemployed and about six hundred soldiers per day returning and looking for work. More and more ex-Wobblies, unemployed workers and soldiers returning home turned to the Communist Party for help.

Inspired by the Russian Revolution of 1917, Harry Wicks, an ex-Wobbly and member of the Communist Labor Party (CLP), began building a large coalition of leftist and labor groups in April 1918. On January 9, 1919, Wicks called for a mass meeting at Arion Hall to form a Portland Council of Workers, Soldiers and Sailors (CWSS). Modeled after the workers' councils, or soviets, of the new Soviet Union, the CWSS was a method of building "industrial democracy" and giving the working class a strong voice in government. Wicks had two main goals: 1) to build a regional workers'

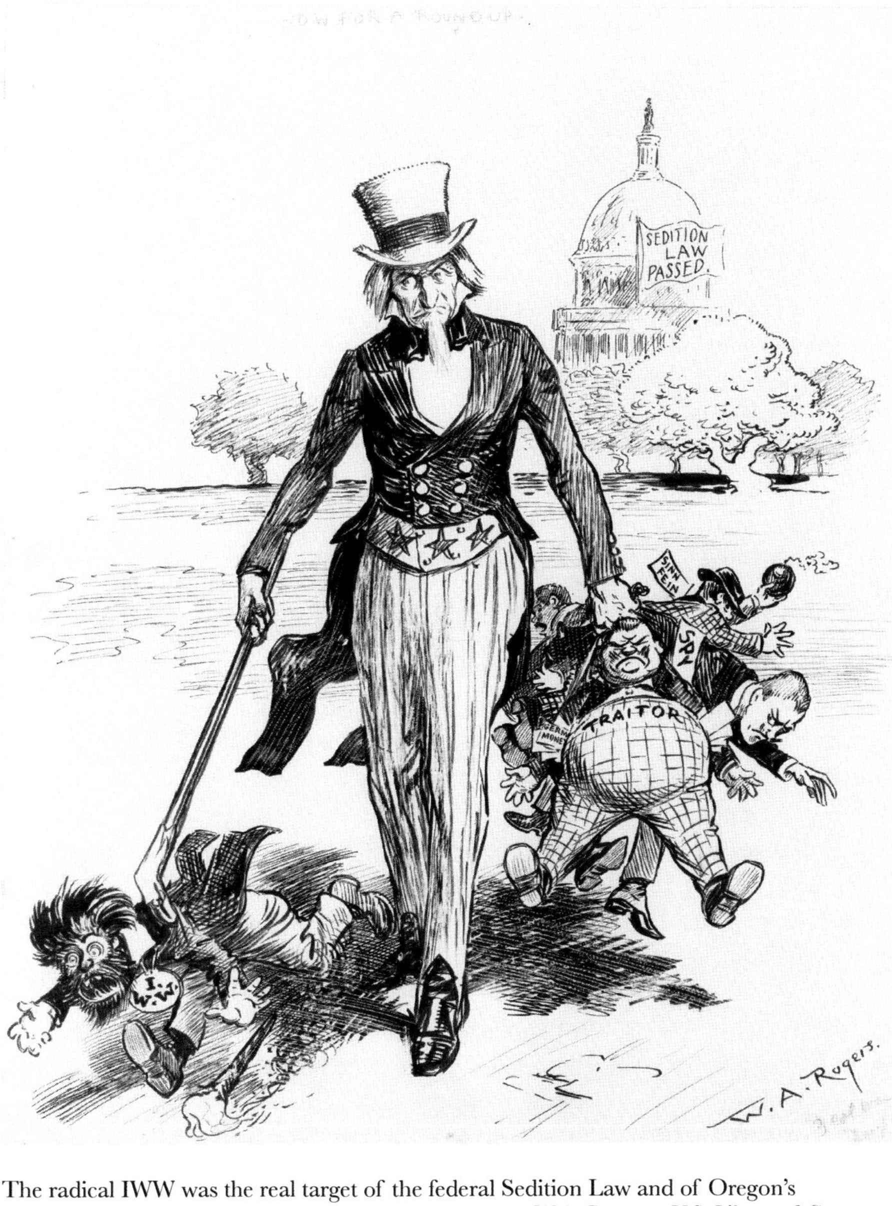


The radical IWW was the real target of the federal Sedition Law and of Oregon's Syndicalism Law, as is clearly shown in this cartoon by W.A. Rogers. *U.S. Library of Congress.*

council in cooperation with councils being set up in Tacoma and Seattle and 2) for working people to take the reins of government and control their own future. The CWSS began to hold lively regular meetings that overflowed the one-thousand-seat Arion Hall.

Mayor Baker and his friends saw the CWSS as a Bolshevik threat to Portland. Baker refused to allow the group to meet at Civic Auditorium, the usual venue for large political meetings, and mobilized the Multnomah Guard, a six-hundred-man paramilitary unit designed to protect the city from radical insurrection. Baker called for passage of a criminal syndicalism bill, saying it was the "greatest need of the day." State senator K.K. Kubli, from southeast Portland, introduced the law and ramrodded it through the legislature before the end of January, prompting the *Oregonian* headline "Legislature Sets Speed Record."

As the criminal syndicalism bill was being pushed through the state legislature in Salem, the situation in Seattle was becoming intense. Seattle's shipbuilding industry had expanded as fast, or faster, than Portland's. By January 1919, there were more than thirty-five thousand people working in Seattle shipyards. Expecting pay raises at the end of the war, the shipyard workers were disappointed to be faced with layoffs and a proposed wage cut. Feeling the growing power of union organizing, the shipyard workers went out on strike at the end of January and called for "sympathy strikes" by workers in other industries.

With support from the Seattle Council of Workers, Soldiers and Sailors and the Central Labor Council, on February 6, all of the city's industries were shut down by the first "general strike" in American history. According to the ideology of the IWW, the general strike was the first step in the revolution in which working people would seize the means of production, as well as the reins of government. With Seattle shut down, it was the job of all loyal Wobblies to spread the strike down the coast and across the nation.

In Seattle, the Central Labor Council elected a General Strike Committee that took control of the city, making sure the hospitals remained open, electricity kept flowing and people could get something to eat. It was the first time in American history that ordinary working people seized control of a city government, and things went surprisingly smoothly in the Emerald City. The general strike lasted only a week and didn't spread outside of Seattle, mostly due to repressive measures taken in other cities, but the strike would be an important turning point and opened a new era of labor organizing and strife.

During the same week that the general strike was declared in Seattle, Oregon's Criminal Syndicalism Bill finally became law. Although the

*Oregonian* warned that the new law was unconstitutional, a fact confirmed by the Supreme Court in 1936, Mayor Baker lost no time in enforcing it anyway. On February 8, Baker ordered sweeps of the streets and the arrest of anyone attempting to distribute "radical literature." George Savoleinen, an IWW organizer suspected by the police of advocating a general strike in Portland, had been picked up the day before the law went into effect. On the eighth, Savoleinen was charged under the new law. That same day, Harlin Talbert, an actor from Albany who served as state secretary for the Socialist Party, and four others were arrested for selling the *Western Socialist* newspaper on the streets of Portland.

The next day, C.E. Brandt, a retired blacksmith, was arrested for carrying a banner advertising the Workers' Industrial Union and a lecture about the General Strike at Alisky Hall. Brandt's arrest led to a raid on the Socialist Labor Party office and a manhunt for the fifteen people on its membership list. That evening, the city council passed an ordinance making it illegal to carry signs, banners or flags to advertise labor unions. The extra law was part of a strategy to harass and discourage labor supporters by arresting them on multiple charges. Sentenced to days or weeks on the rock pile and multiple fines, labor organizers were kept broke and discouraged. Portland's reputation as a hard town for working people remained intact.

The next step was to stop socialists from holding public meetings. The police warned the landlords of Arion Hall and the building where the IWW rented offices that unless the radicals were evicted, the landlords themselves would face prosecution under the Syndicalism Law. Mayor Baker had Harry Wicks, president of the Council of Workers, Soldiers and Sailors (CWSS) and editor of the *Western Socialist*, hauled into his office. Baker, police chief Nelson Johnson and U.S. Bureau of Investigation agent William Bryon warned Wicks of the danger he was running and suggested that he get out of town. Wicks, who was later accused of being a police informant, attempted to influence the CWSS to hold a recall election for Mayor Baker, but many radicals, including Dr. Marie Equi, felt it was more important to stage a general strike in sympathy with Seattle. As CWSS meetings became more contentious and less productive, Wicks finally resigned as president and then left town. If he was trying to avoid prosecution, it didn't work. A few days later, he was arrested in Spokane and quickly convicted under Washington's new Syndicalism Law.

In what the *Oregonian* called a type of "recurring festivity," the IWW Hall was raided by the police and vigilantes who seized its membership list and destroyed everything else in the office. The Wobblies were evicted, and

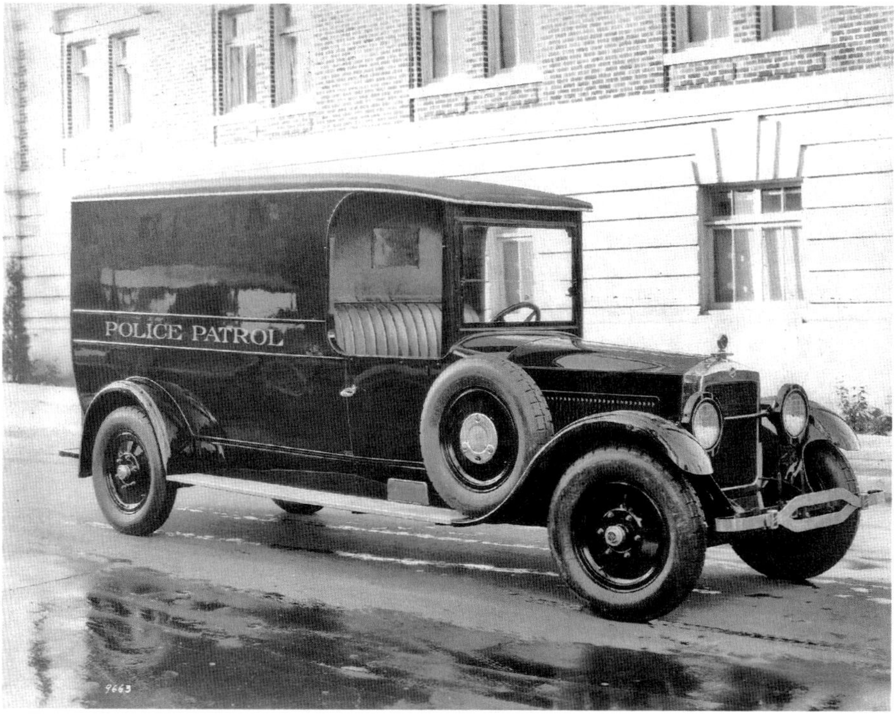


A ride in the paddy wagon, code name 99, was a common experience for supporters of labor unions in the 1920s. Every police officer carried a key for the callboxes placed at strategic points, where they could call to have prisoners picked up. *Portland City Archive.*

several of them were arrested. The Wobblies weren't completely defenseless, though. In an inspired move, Portland's IWW leaders wrote letters to city officials and local pastors, giving the addresses of thirteen locations where illegal alcohol was being sold. The IWW placed pickets around the speakeasies and announced a boycott of their illegal product. Although the police bureau wasn't handling liquor distribution yet, the revelation of illegal drinking parlors being allowed to operate openly was highly embarrassing, and the police backed off from the Wobblies, at least for the short term.

# CHAPTER 5
# THE POWER TO CONTROL

*So in the end the law will have reached nowhere—being defeated by its own stupidity.*
*—Oregonian*

H.R. Edmunds, aka the Tillamook Kid, boarded the Southern Pacific Cascade Express at the Oakland Depot in early 1918, bound for Portland. It was a comfortable overnight trip in a Pullman car, and Edmunds would arrive in Portland late in the morning. Even though he was on an illegal mission, accompanying three trunks of bootleg liquor, he felt secure and wasn't worried about the law. Before departing, he had given his partner, Donald Nix, thirty-five dollars to "fix" the police in Portland. Nix allegedly told him that Sergeant Sammy Vessey had been fixed and would see that everything was okay. The Pullman porters who served passengers were doing the smuggling. Edmunds, son of a prominent Oregon businessman and one of the bootlegging ring's leaders, was just observing the operation; he wasn't connected to the trunks until many months later. At Union Depot in Portland, a porter collected the trunks at the baggage department, loaded them onto his cart and wheeled them across the cavernous waiting room. As the porter's cart approached the front door, uniformed police sergeant Ben Wade motioned for the porter to stop. Wade was suspicious about the luggage and wanted to do a "shake and sniff test." The police bureau was maintaining that no warrant was necessary if a piece of luggage couldn't pass this test. Sergeant Sammy Vessey waved his fellow officer off, saying that he had already checked those trunks and they were loaded into a hired car at the curb. This is the story Edmunds told at his federal trial in San Francisco later that year; many thought he was lying.

Despite charges of corruption, the War Emergency Squad, also known as the morals squad, and Sheriff Thomas Hurlburt continued to fight the illegal liquor trade. Liquor from California, Canada and Chicago continued to flow into Portland by train, boat and car. The Southern Pacific (SP) Railroad, with the connivance of the Pullman porters, continued to bring large shipments into the city. The SP and baggage officials at Union Depot

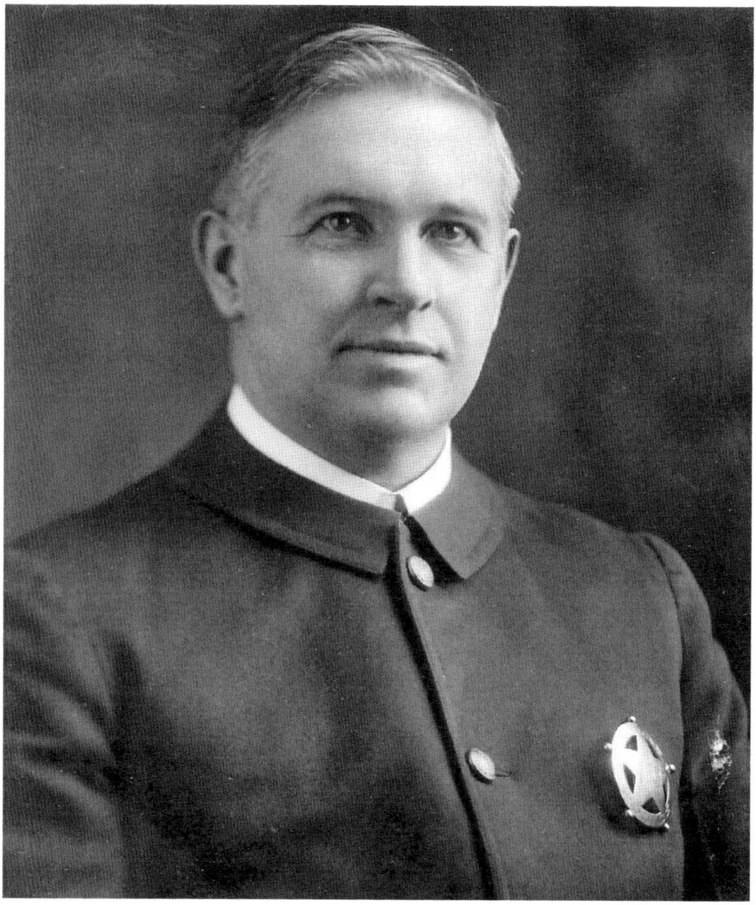

Sammy Vessey was charged with aiding bootleggers in 1918. He was exonerated of charges and retired from the police bureau in 1931. His record of liquor seizures was impressive, and it is possible that bootleggers tried to frame him because of his effectiveness. *Portland Police Historical Society.*

refused to cooperate with the police, who insisted they needed no search warrant to search luggage. Employing the "shake and sniff" method, sheriff's deputies listened for tell-tale gurgling or sniffed for whiskey fumes from broken bottles. Using these methods, the police seized gallons of illegal booze, but many of the cases were thrown out of court as judges attempted to clarify search and seizure laws.

When things got too hot at the Union Depot, the porters started unloading their cargo at rural stations, and then operatives of the ring would drive the contraband into Portland by car. Pullman porters on the Northern Pacific line, coming to Portland from Chicago by way of Minneapolis, brought in loads of liquor as well, unloading at the eastside depot. Both Pullman porter rings, whether they operated separately or in concert, subverted police officers to help them.

Many officers were charged with helping bootleggers. In some cases, such as that of patrolman Sam Vessey, the charges may have been false. Vessey was particularly adept at locating trunks full of booze at the Union Depot, but bootlegger H.R. Edmunds (aka the Tillamook Kid) claimed that Vessey allowed him to bring several trunks full of liquor out of the station, telling other officers that he had searched them already. Edmunds claimed that his partner, Donald Nix, had "fixed" Vessey. It is possible that Vessey had inside information on shipments and made seizures to keep his record clean, but his liquor seizures were numerous and the bootleggers may have been trying to neutralize an effective enemy. It can be very difficult, especially after so many years, to decipher the truth behind various charges against police officers. Vessey was exonerated of charges in 1919 and then transferred from the morals squad. He was one of the founding members of the new auto theft squad and had a long career with the police bureau, retiring in 1931.

Even if the charges against Vessey were an attempt to get rid of an efficient officer, it is clear that several other officers did give in to the temptations offered by bootleggers. For example, motorcycle officer Roy C. Brown, was arrested after being observed twice picking up suitcases at the eastside railroad depot. The second time, Brown was arrested with twelve quarts of whiskey in the suitcase he had picked up. Brown claimed that the liquor was evidence that he was taking downtown, but no one believed him. He was dismissed from the police bureau and spent time in jail.

It is interesting to note that all of the officers charged with this crime came either from the morals squad or the motorcycle division. Many of them ended up working in the traffic division under Captain Frank Ervin. Sometimes charges against officers were motivated by politics or even

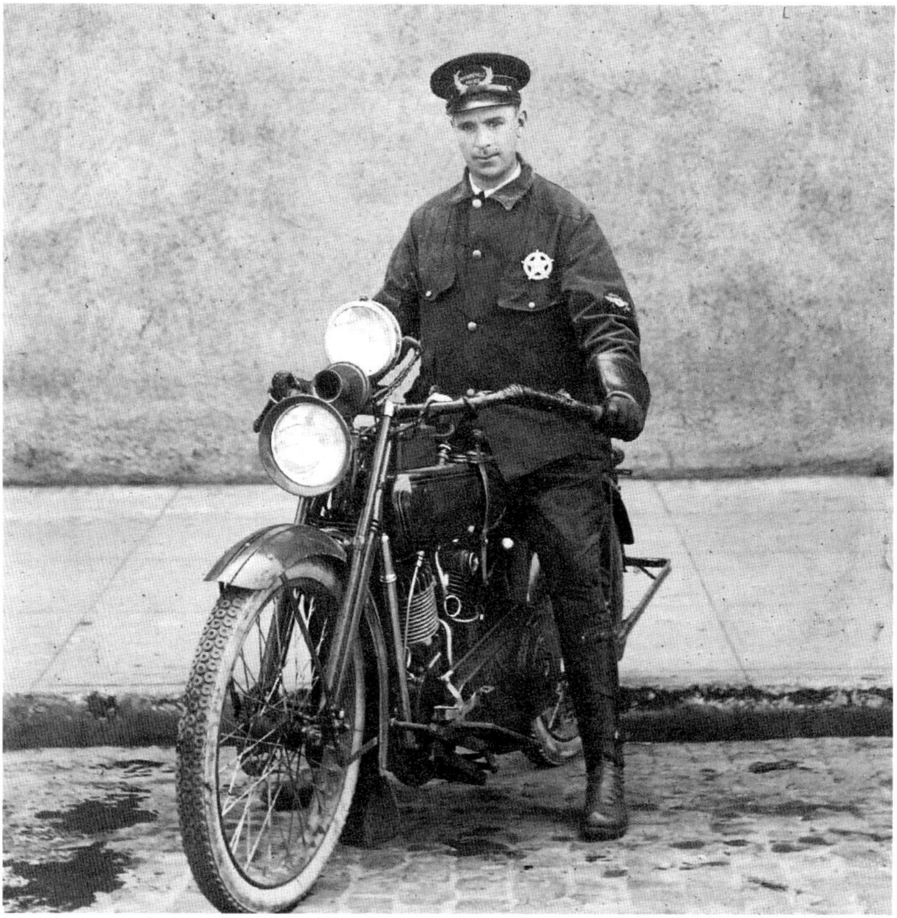

Frank Ervin served with Harry Coulter on the motorcycle squad when Coulter was convicted of bootlegging. Six years later, Ervin reinstated Coulter to the police bureau and served as his commander in the traffic division. *Portland Police Historical Society.*

personal animosity. For example, Lieutenant Leo Harms, the head of the War Emergency Squad, was charged with drinking and gambling on duty and drunken reckless gunplay in 1918. The two officers who charged Lieutenant Harms with these crimes were both dismissed from the bureau, and one of them, Anson Long, was later convicted of impersonating an officer and stealing liquor from bootleggers. Long eventually confessed that he brought charges against Harms for revenge, and Harms was exonerated. Harms took over the traffic division but resigned from the force in 1928, with full retirement benefits, after another scandal involving an affair with a married woman called into question his earlier exoneration. The case of Leo Harms illustrates the difficulty of sorting out the truth of charges against police officers.

A conviction for bootlegging did not necessarily mean the end of a police officer's career. The case of Harry Coulter, another motorcycle officer, is a good example. In 1919, Coulter and Officer Fred Schmidtke, a morals squad officer, were charged with landing a boatload of liquor at Linnton. The two officers had been involved with the high-profile seizure of liquor from a boat less than a month earlier. The previous case may have given them the idea to go into business for themselves. Both men were convicted of bootlegging and served short terms in jail after being cashiered from the police bureau. In 1925, Coulter was reinstated as a policeman and served in the traffic division under Captain Frank Ervin, with whom he had served on the motorcycle squad. By that time, the police bureau was supervising most of the liquor distribution in Portland, and Ervin was Chief Leon Jenkins's right-hand man, handling liquor distribution and anti-union activity, along with a lot of other dirty work.

Portland was not the only city that had a problem with police involved in bootlegging. Officers in Pendleton, Medford, Astoria and Madras were charged with that crime. Washington County sheriff Jesse Applegate was forced to resign after being convicted of bootlegging and then served a term in prison for his crimes. In Seattle, the mayor and the chief of police were indicted for cooperating with the Billingsley brothers in their bootlegging enterprise, and the mayor of Los Angeles was indicted for similar crimes. Portland police chief Nelson Johnson claimed that manpower shortages caused by the war forced him to hire officers who were unfit for duty and susceptible to corruption. The excuse by Johnson was ridiculous; by 1917, the dominant culture of "pay for service" combined with abysmally low pay had made corruption systemic in the police bureau.

Mayor Baker must have observed all of this with concern as he made plans to take over bootlegging in Portland. His election as mayor would not necessarily keep him out of jail if things went wrong. What he needed was a loyal team who could insulate him from responsibility and handle things competently on its own. In 1919, he appointed Captain Leon Jenkins as police chief. Jenkins, who had walked a beat in the North End as a rookie and served as the third leader of the War Emergency Squad, was an excellent choice. Jenkins was an able and popular chief who managed to oversee liquor distribution while continuing high-profile raids that reduced competition and guarded the city's reputation for law enforcement. Another member of Baker's team was Augustine Ardiss, better known as Bobby Evans. Evans, who had been a popular boxer before being appointed "matchmaker" by the Portland Boxing Commission, grew up in the immigrant neighborhood of South Portland and knew the mayor well from their membership in the Ex-Newsboys' Association. Evans had great skill at recruiting muscle from among the young Italian and Jewish boxers and basketball players at the Neighborhood House Community Center. Young men such as Abe Weinstein, Jake Minsky and the DePinto brothers were just a few of the people who found opportunity in "Matchmaker" Bobby's operation. Evans managed to keep peaceful relations with Al Capone's outfit, which supplied much of the liquor and all of the coin-operated machines in Portland, while keeping the national mob from establishing a foothold here. With Jenkins and Evans, Baker had both sides of the law effectively covered.

The first move of Baker's organization was to neutralize the Pullman porters' ring. Railroads were one of the most common means of smuggling liquor into Portland, and there were a number of gangs and individuals who used them. One gang, which has never been identified, used freight

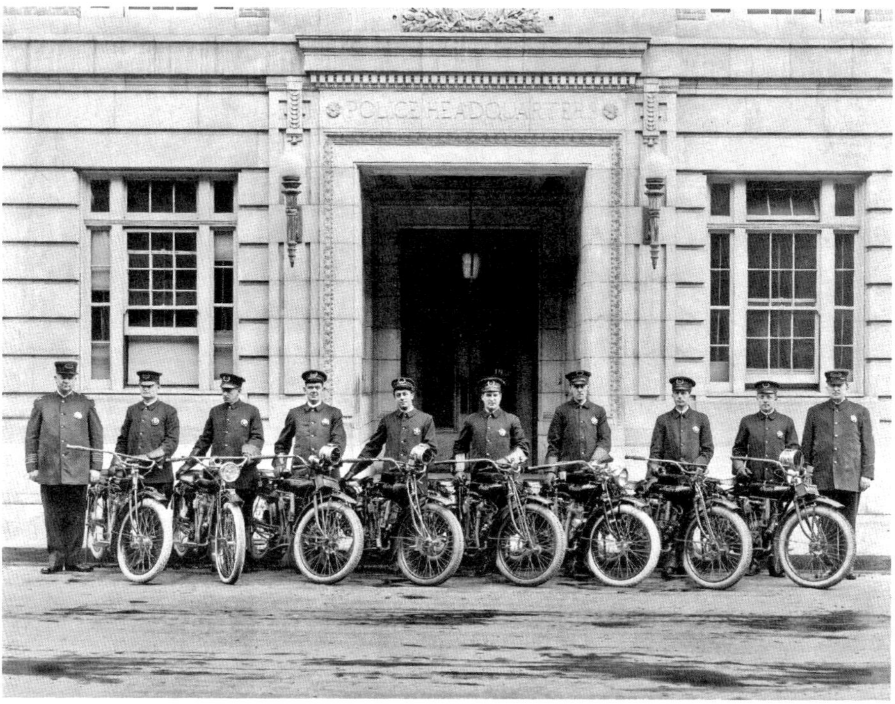

The first Portland motorcycle patrol was organized in 1915. Motorcycle officers enforced traffic laws and guarded the toll booth on the Interstate Bridge. *Portland Police Historical Society.*

shipments of "household goods" to bring in gallons of whiskey. Although a number of their shipments were seized, no arrests were made. Several small-time bootleggers brought liquor into Portland in their luggage. Some of them were caught, but it is likely that many of them got away with it. The most successful and persistent bootleggers to use railroads worked with the Pullman porters who worked the rail lines. Working with William Allen and Al Green of the Golden West Hotel, the Pullman porter ring was the most dependable source of high-quality whiskey in the Pacific Northwest.

Originally under the leadership of John Lowe and Sam "Yam" Wallace, the ring included Pullman porters such as Lawrence Tucker, William Fonville and Edward Allen, William Allen's brother. These men got quite rich in a short time. Many of them spent money on big, powerful cars and lived like kings on the fifth floor of the Golden West. Fonville, who was more taken with automobiles than most, died in a traffic accident near Chehalis, Washington, in 1920. Working most of his life for nickel and dime tips, Fonville left a personal estate of over $50,000 ($580,000 in 2015). Edward Allen, who kept a low profile, probably managed to get out of the criminal life, since he disappeared from the record. Yam Wallace, whose large maroon touring car was a familiar sight around the North End, struggled with Lowe for leadership of the ring and by 1920 had pushed him out, making himself the undisputed leader. John Lowe, excluded from the Pullman porters' ring continued in bootlegging, but his real interest was armed robbery. Recruiting strong-arm men, both black and white, Lowe used the Read Hotel, across the street from Lownsdale Square, as his headquarters for armed robberies that targeted high-rollers in the bootlegging life like James "Birdlegs" Reed. The conflict between Wallace and Lowe was caused by the power vacuum created by a series of arrests in March 1918.

Sheriff Hurlburt and the morals squad kept the pressure on with regular raids on Union Depot. Fighting both the Southern Pacific Railroad and the Union Depot Baggage Department, both of whom challenged the police's right to search luggage, the sheriff's department seized hundreds of quarts of contraband booze and made dozens of arrests. Most of the arrestees were Pullman porters who easily paid their fines and went back to work. Eventually, the police built a case, and by cooperating with U.S. attorney Barnett Goldstein, they arrested the ring's top leadership in San Francisco, Portland and Salem.

Although national Prohibition hadn't gone into effect, it was against federal law to transport liquor across state lines into dry states. Wartime laws also greatly restricted both the manufacture and sale of intoxicating liquor.

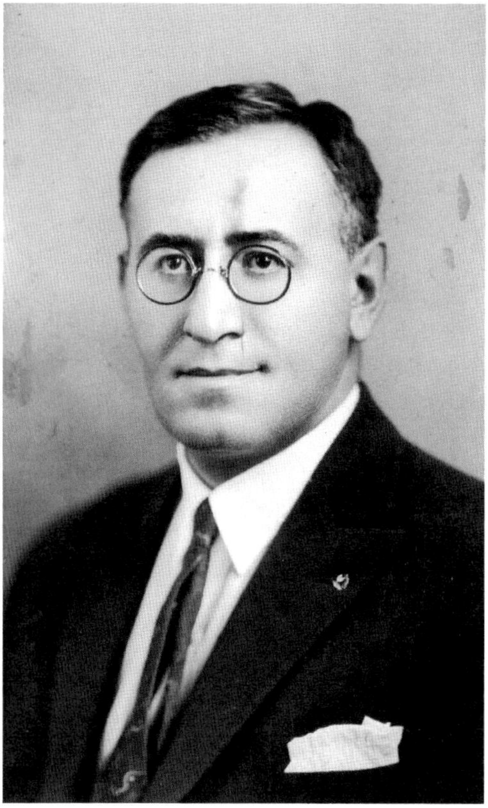

U.S. attorney Barnett Goldstein was the prosecutor who arrested twenty-nine members of the top leadership of the Pullman porters ring in 1918. Although some of the suspects went to jail and their illegal activity was exposed, the ring continued to supply Portland with liquor well into the 1950s. *Portland City Archive.*

Even without these laws, federal agents were happy to cooperate with local police in stopping bootlegging. On March 5, 1918, U.S. attorney Barnett Goldstein ordered coordinated raids in San Francisco, Portland and Salem. Twenty-nine people were arrested, and Goldstein announced that they were the top leadership of two separate rings that had been using the Southern Pacific Railroad to smuggle liquor. Among those arrested were H.R. Edmunds (aka the Tillamook Kid), the son of a prominent businessman; J. Davidson, owner of the Blue Ribbon Brewing Company of San Francisco; and Frank J. Lepsic, owner and proprietor of the Bohemian Liquor Company of San Francisco. The other ring, later known as the Hunt Ring, was led by Walter "the Fox" Hardy and William Hunt of the Hunt Liquor Company of San Francisco. Several others, including employees of the liquor companies and the Southern Pacific Railroad, as well as taxi drivers and independent baggage handlers in all three cities, were swept up in the raids. Some of the charges were dropped as lower-level bootleggers made deals with the prosecutors. The *Oregonian* speculated that the actual leaders of the rings were unnamed "higher ups" in both Portland and San Francisco who were taking the huge profits that these rings were bringing in.

With the leadership of the ring in jail but the liquor still flowing over the railroad lines, the large profits to be made created a struggle for control of the group. John Lowe was quickly pushed out, and Yam Wallace established

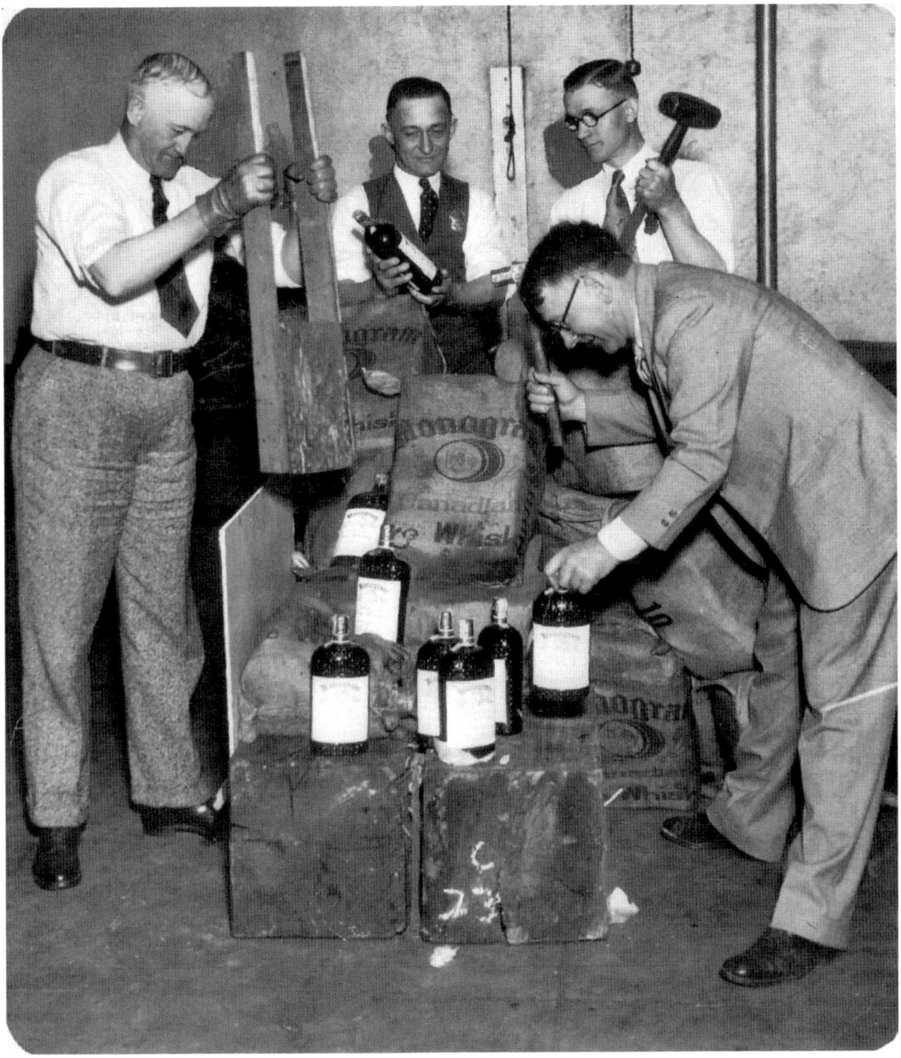

The morals squad was reorganized after the Great War and continued to make liquor raids for propaganda purposes. Soon, the police bureau itself would be the most significant distributor of liquor in Portland. *Oregon Historical Society.*

undisputed leadership of the ring in Portland. Wallace was not cooperative with the police, and he was known for violence in enforcing his leadership, especially against women. Wallace was a large man with a fearsome reputation, and he ran the porters' ring ruthlessly. Although brutal, Wallace had high standards and a good sense of humor. In October 1920, after he had been arrested with a few bottles of whiskey in his possession, Wallace's attorney told

Judge George Rossman in police court that his client deserved a medal instead of a fine. "He is the first bootlegger in many weeks who has produced genuine, bonded liquor instead of moonshine," his attorney explained.

Wallace had a reputation not only as a "bad actor" but also as "the craftiest bootlegger" in Portland. He pioneered the use of "handflasks"—small flasks that held about four tablespoons of liquor, could be concealed in the hand and sold, very profitably, for fifty cents. His employees, especially Tom Johnson and William Fonville, were very adept at hiding shipments of whiskey, often burying it in gardens or hiding it under side or backyard woodpiles. Johnson was once arrested wearing a long overcoat with twelve pints of whiskey hanging inside it on strings.

Tom Johnson, the son of ex-slaves from Louisiana, became one of the most successful and prominent members of Portland's African American community in a career that spanned more than five decades. Rumored to have been involved with an armed robbery gang in California, Johnson had plenty of money when he arrived in Portland in 1910. It didn't take him long before he had established a gambling and drinking club in northwest Portland, called the Orpheus Club. Gambling seems to have been Johnson's passion. In the 1940s and 1950s, when he was a successful realtor and property developer, the Williams Avenue office of his realty company, Keystone Investments, had a secret entrance to the Keystone Club, one of the city's most luxurious gambling dens. Gambling has always gone hand in hand with drinking and prostitution in Portland, and Johnson was involved with all of it. In 1918, after returning from service in the Great War, he organized the Porters' Club and soon got involved with the smuggling of the Pullman porters' ring.

In 1920, Johnson saw opportunity in the misfortune of his boss, Yam Wallace. The profitable Pullman porters' ring had attracted the attention of a Kansas City mob that sent three "hard-boiled niggers"—a direct quote from the *Oregonian*—to challenge Wallace's leadership. Wallace was humiliated in a confrontation with the Kansas City muscle on Everett Street in front of the Golden West Hotel. The men forced Wallace to run down the street, kicking him repeatedly on the backside as he attempted to flee. Wallace's reputation for being tough was broken with the humiliation, and a rift between him and Tom Johnson was created when Johnson laughed at his plight and openly shared the story around town, gleefully regaling his listeners with colorful details. Wallace tried to reassert his authority by confronting war veteran Johnson, who, wielding a straight razor, cut him badly in "the regions where the parental razor strop is frequently applied."

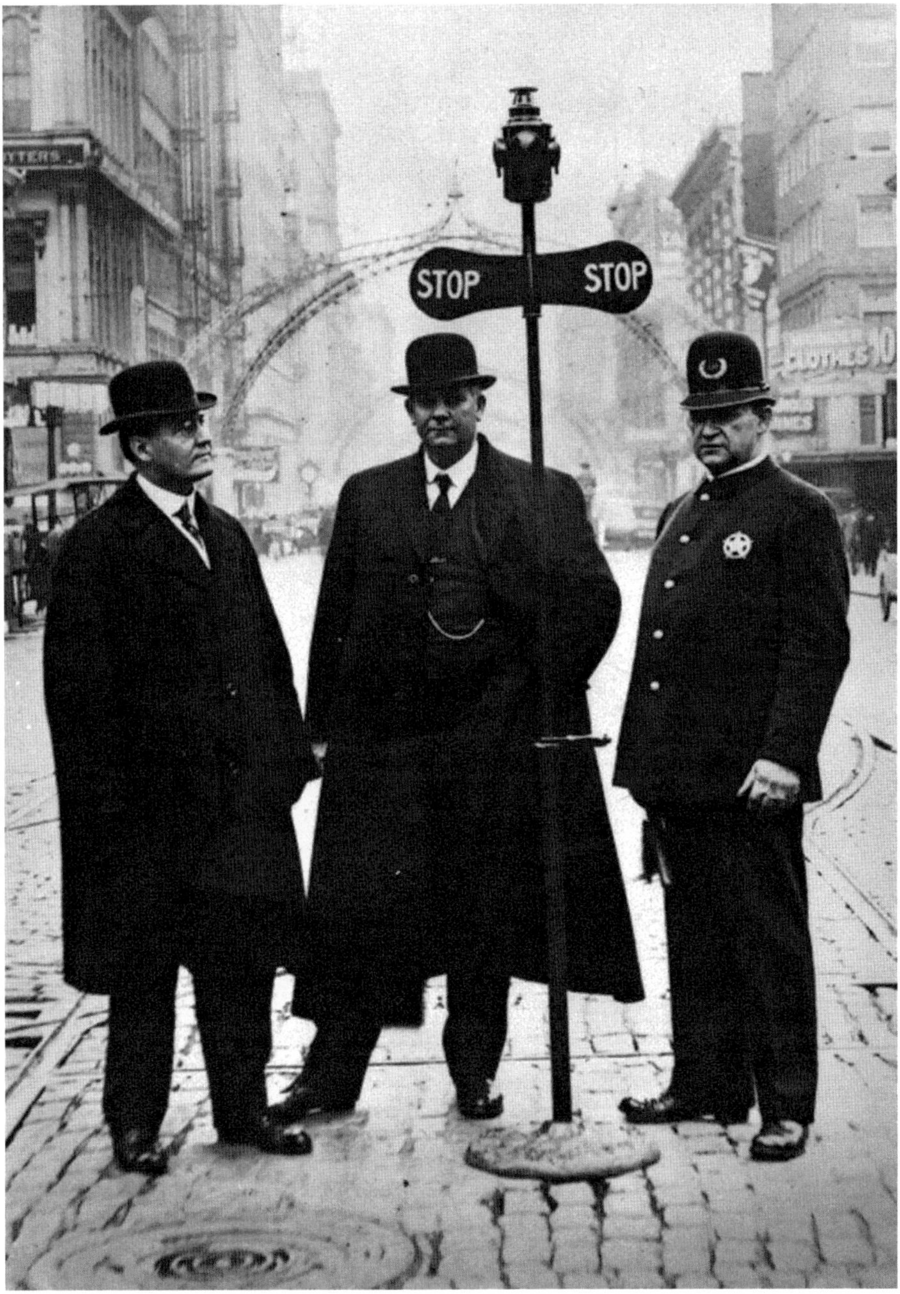


Mayor H. Russell Albee (right) installed the first traffic signal in 1915, and by 1920 traffic had become a serious issue in Portland. Captain Frank Ervin of the traffic division wielded great power in enforcing the traffic laws. *Portland City Archive.*

Wallace, infuriated and further humiliated, threatened Johnson's life from his hospital bed. The city police quickly arrested Wallace for issuing threats, and a couple of weeks later, after his release, Wallace was caught with forty ounces of cocaine with a street value of nearly $10,000 ($118,000 in 2015). He was sent to McNeil Island Penitentiary for a long prison term. Tom Johnson took over control of the Pullman porters' ring and used it as the base to build his power in Portland. In later years, Johnson was well known for his close relationship with the city government and local crime bosses Jim Elkins and Al Winter. It is hardly a stretch to imagine that he made a deal with the police bureau and continued operating the bootlegging ring under police supervision. Arrested more than fifty times, under several different names, during his long career Johnson never faced serious jail time and obviously enjoyed special protection from the Portland police. Johnson died in 1964, a very wealthy man after his well-timed investments in property essential to the Memorial Coliseum project and the Emmanuel Hospital project. The *Oregonian* glossed over his involvement in the underworld, saying, "Although he was deeply involved in Portland night life, Mr. Johnson was one of those passing institutions—a Negro leader who tried to bridge the gap between members of his race in trouble with the law and the city's White officialdom."

Police chief Leon Jenkins was busy in the early years of his administration gaining control of the bootlegging in Portland, but Mayor Baker was still anxious to "exterminate" all of the radicals in town. Balancing priorities, and fully conscious of the public relations problem the IWW presented with its knowledge of the bootlegging situation, Jenkins chose to seize his opportunities where they presented themselves. The IWW kept up resistance to the Syndicalism Law with a campaign of civil disobedience. Dr. Marie Equi was arrested in March 1919 for distributing IWW literature on the streets. She claimed that she was trying to recruit ex-soldiers to continue passing out literature because they were the only ones not afraid to go up against the police. In June, a series of bombings on the East Coast, including one that exploded on the front porch of Attorney General A. Mitchell Palmer's home, gave the police another chance to hit the IWW. Raiding the IWW hall in northwest Portland, the police seized boxes of literature and arrested John Johnson and fourteen other Wobblies. When they couldn't be connected to the East Coast bombings, the men were sentenced to the rock pile for vagrancy and other "crimes."

The next opportunity to hit the Wobblies presented itself in November 1919 during the celebration of the nation's first Armistice Day holiday. The IWW had been attempting to rebuild its power in southwest Washington by organizing workers in the coal mining industry in Chehalis and Centralia, about sixty miles north of Portland. In Portland and other communities of the Pacific Northwest, the Wobblies were strongly opposed by veterans' groups. The Veterans of Foreign Wars and the Spanish-American War Veterans often participated with the police in putting down IWW gatherings and raiding their offices. Returning veterans of the Great War founded a new organization, the American Legion (AL), which not only had greater numbers than any other veterans' group but also was completely dedicated to white supremacy and reactionary politics. In Centralia, Washington, the AL had taken the lead in activity against the IWW and raided its offices as vigilantes several times, destroying furniture and records and beating any Wobblies they could catch. With the celebration of Armistice Day, members of the AL planned to march in a large parade in their uniforms. Wobblies knew that the AL would take the opportunity to raid their office again. Some of the Wobblies were war veterans themselves, and they made detailed plans to defend their office if the AL should decide to attack again.

Whether by coincidence or on purpose, the AL contingent of the parade was scheduled to mark time in front of the IWW Hall as the parade closed ranks. There is much dispute about the events that occurred during the parade, which has come to be known as the Centralia Massacre. What is clear is that at some point an order was given to the AL marchers who were marking time. A group of them broke ranks and rushed the door of the IWW Hall. Several armed Wobblies were stationed inside the building, and at least two sharpshooters with high-powered rifles were stationed on a hill a short distance away. Dr. Frank Bickford, one of the marching AL members, later admitted that he led the raid and that the door of the IWW Hall was kicked in before the shooting started. The raiding party and the rest of the AL contingent were caught in a deadly crossfire between the armed Wobblies in the hall and the sharpshooters on Seminary Hill. Three of them, including attorney and AL commander Warren Grimm, were killed. The surviving AL marchers rushed the hall, and several of them were wounded before the armed Wobblies inside were overwhelmed and gave up. Wesley Everest, a Portland Wobbly from Newberg, ran out the back door and, armed with a handgun, led a running gunfight toward the Skookumchuck River, where he killed AL member Dale Hubbard before being captured and severely beaten.

A dozen Wobblies were arrested and held in the Centralia jail to face murder charges, but that night during a mysterious electric power blackout, a mob abducted Everest from his jail cell. The mob drove the IWW member in a large car to a bridge over the Chehalis River, where they took out a knife and castrated him before hanging him from the bridge. The massacre was used as justification for a series of raids on IWW and Communist offices and mass arrests of radicals all over the country. In Portland on the evening of November 11, spies from the newly formed "red squad" under the command of Lieutenant Harvey Thatcher infiltrated a meeting of the Council of Workers, Soldiers and Sailors. The spies got word back to Thatcher that "sedition" was being spoken, and he surrounded the building with a squadron headed by Sergeant Frank Ervin. Ervin, Thatcher and several other officers in plain clothes infiltrated the crowd and arrested fifty-three people, charging them with vagrancy. Among those arrested was Joseph Laundy, a candidate for president of the Central Labor Council. That evening, police began rounding up anyone who admitted to supporting the IWW. Mayor Baker said it was the duty of the police bureau to lock the radicals up for their own protection.

Within a couple of days, the jail on the top floors of the county courthouse was overflowing with prisoners. Mayor Baker called for reopening the rock pile at Kelley Butte and started making renovations so the old stockade that had been closed there could be reopened to house prisoners. Hundreds of Wobblies, communists and socialists were arrested, and after the Palmer raids in January 1920, nearly one hundred radicals were deported from the Portland area. Others, American citizens, were sentenced to hard labor for various crimes, including vagrancy, sodomy and possession of IWW literature. The IWW was forced deeper underground, and the Communist Labor Party, although harassed just as badly as the IWW, benefited from new members and a stronger commitment to organizing against the government repression.

## CHAPTER 6

# HIGHLY ORGANIZED CRIME

*I keep two bank accounts so in case one goes broke I won't be washed out.*
*–George Baker*

The Sells-Floto Circus performance in Vancouver, Washington, on the night of September 16, 1921, was well received. It featured more than seventy-five separate acts, fifty-seven clowns and what the circus's press agent called the "greatest act playing under the big top today," the Riding Hannefords—a family of trick riders featuring "Poodles" Hanneford, the trick-riding clown. The act that really dazzled the crowd that night was the "slack wire" routine of Berta Beeson, a former grocery clerk from Indiana whose real name was Herbert Beeson. Beeson dressed as a woman for his act, and very few in the audience could tell the difference. Crime often followed the circus on its travels, but the 1921 season was more crime-plagued than most; in Baker, Oregon, that summer, two prisoners escaped from the city jail during the circus parade that preceded the first performance. In Vancouver, after the last performance, crime struck again.

It was the regular weekly payday for the circus crew so there was more money on hand than usual as F.A. McLane, the circus treasurer, loaded up the "treasure wagon"—a large truck—to transport the box office take to the "treasure car" on the circus's train that was parked in the Vancouver train yard. Five members of the Hanneford family, including Poodles and his mother, Grace, the family matriarch, were riding with McLane, his assistant Robert de Lochte and Mike Grace, the driver, as the truck left the circus grounds. When the truck entered a clump of woods on the way to the rail yards, two shots were fired from the trees, and two men jumped out, ordering the truck to stop and all of the people to get out.

Grace Hanneford was uncooperative from the start; she refused to get out of the truck as the others were lined up along the side of the road. She argued with the robbers, and they finally agreed that because of her age she could stay in the truck as long as she kept her hands up. The robbers searched each person, taking jewelry and other belongings. McLane had $600 in cash and several checks on him, which the robbers took. Finally, the robbers searched the truck and found the money bag, which contained more than $4,000 in cash and over $20,000 in bank drafts and checks. The robbers ordered Grace out of the truck finally and began searching her. Poodles the clown objected to the robbers' rough treatment of his mother, and one of them hit him in the head with a pistol, knocking him out. Grace began to fight with the robber searching her, and she was knocked out as well. In an act of spite, the robbers took Grace's handbag and glasses before fleeing in a stolen Hupmobile driven by a third robber.

The two robbers who handled the crowd were later identified as Roy Moore, an ex-logger from Portland who had recently moved to Seattle with his wife and two daughters, and Ben Orcutt, a veteran criminal, bootlegger and cocaine smuggler. The third robber, known only as D. Rasor, was never found. Witnesses after the robbery told of a struggle in the getaway car and a shot being fired. At least one witness saw the third robber limp away, and police followed a blood trail for several blocks but never found the man. It would not be the last time that Roy Moore shot one of his accomplices during a robbery. Moore and Orcutt stopped somewhere to pick up Bess Moore and her two daughters, Edna and Florine, and Orcutt's companion, Christine Gross, before driving north. They stopped at an empty spot just short of La Center and buried the loot in the woods before continuing on to Seattle.

Two days later, Orcutt and Moore were wounded by Vancouver police officers when they attempted to recover the loot from its hiding place; a local farmer had stumbled upon the partially buried money bag and alerted the police, who staked out the woods near La Center. Bess Moore and Christine Gross were arrested as material witnesses, and the two little girls were also taken into custody. It was the biggest crime so far of a long criminal career for Roy Moore, who would gain the moniker "King of the Northwest Bootleggers" before serving a term at McNeil Island Penitentiary and returning to armed robbery after the end of prohibition. The wide-

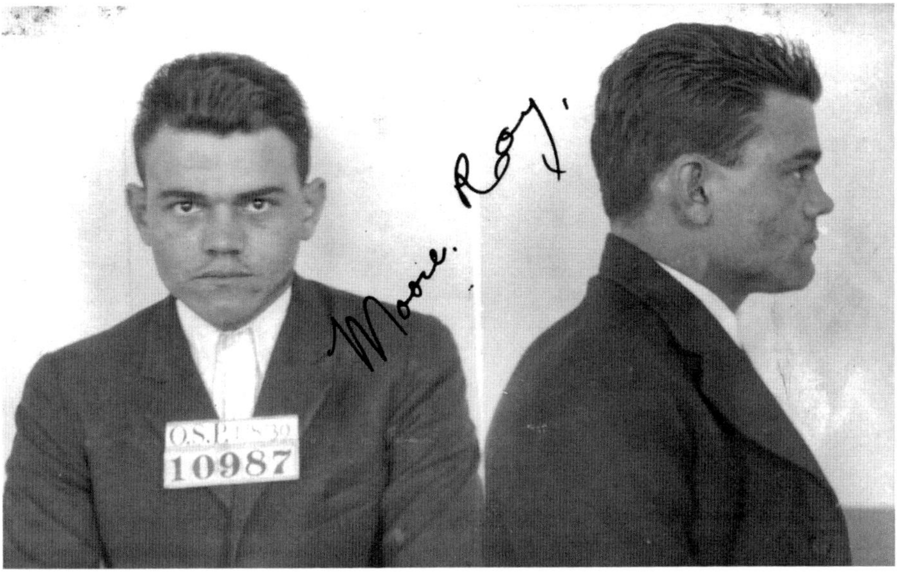


If this is the correct Roy Moore, it is one of the only known photos of the one-time "King of the Northwest Bootleggers" and the architect of the 1945 triple robbery at Brownsville, Oregon. This mug shot is for an arrest in Coos Bay, where he robbed a store because he was broke. *Oregon State Archive.*

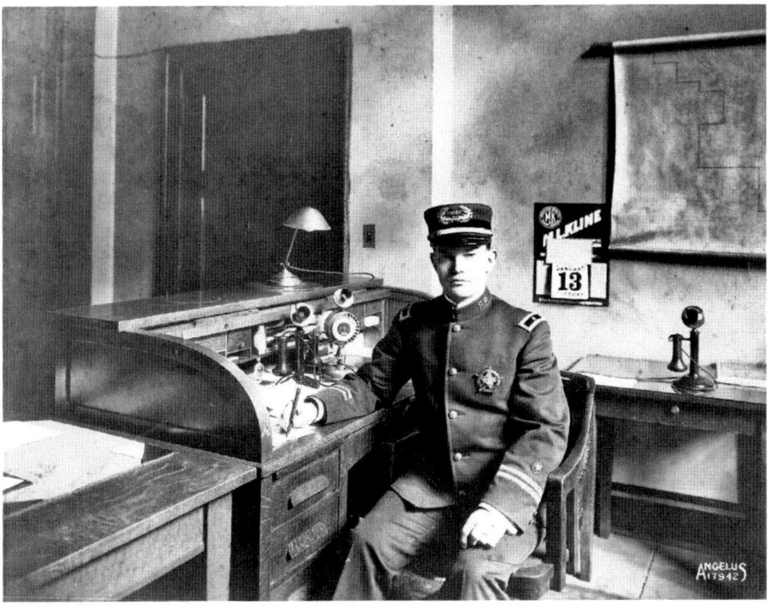


Leon Jenkins became chief of police in 1919, just a couple of months before this picture was taken. He joined the police bureau in 1908 and walked a beat in "Coontown" near Union Depot before rising through the ranks. *Portland Police Historical Society.*

open North End of Portland, with its protected criminal element, made the Rose City a comfortable headquarters for criminal gangs. Roy Moore was just one of the ambitious criminals who made Portland their home and the base of their operations throughout the Pacific Northwest.

Around the same time as the Sells-Floto Circus robbery, Frank Kodat, a safecracker from Washington State, was sentenced to a term in the Oregon State Penitentiary for a burglary gone wrong in a Gold Hill, Oregon bank. A natural networker, Kodat, who would acquire the moniker "Shy Frank," made many of the contacts in prison that would make him the successful leader of an armed robbery ring based in southeast Portland. When Kodat was released in 1925, he made Portland his home, purchasing a building on Southeast Water Street near the Willamette River. He got his moniker "Shy Frank" because he avoided publicity, but there was one thing he wanted everyone to know: he was going straight, and he wanted to help other ex-cons live honest lives.

Kodat opened his building as a boardinghouse for ex-cons who wanted a new start. What he didn't say was that the building included a speakeasy, where you could get an illegal drink and meet friendly "working girls," and the boardinghouse was the headquarters for a criminal gang that pulled burglaries and armed robberies all over the West Coast. Kodat, who had serious health problems, retired as a safecracker, or yegg, and served as the "brains" of the gang, teaching less experienced crooks his skills and providing a protected place for them to lay low between jobs. Kodat's main rule: no jobs in Portland.

Frank Kodat built a powerful gang that included robbers, gunmen and pimps on both sides of the river. Like many of Portland's bootleggers, liquor was a sideline for Kodat: an easy source of income that could support his bigger schemes. Kodat enforced his will ruthlessly, relying on "fingermen" like Jake Silverman and "buttonmen" like Jack Crim, to dispose of rule breakers. Kodat's relationship with, and regular payments to, Bobby Evans gave him protection from the police. Even when his role in the murder of Jimmy Walker and Edith McLain was exposed in 1933, Kodat faced no consequences. His underling, Jake Silverman, who had driven the car involved in the double murder, took the rap and spent three years in jail.

Bootlegging was a sideline for John Lowe as well. Booted out of his leadership position in the Pullman porters' ring and surviving more than one attempt on his life, Lowe recruited a gang of armed robbers to help him get his revenge. Using the run-down transient Read Hotel, only a block from the Multnomah County Courthouse, as headquarters, Lowe's gang targeted other bootleggers, especially those supplied by the Pullman porters' ring, for its victims. For example, Lowe was the mastermind of the notorious raid on Birdlegs's roadhouse in 1926. Lowe's relationship with the police, especially with Captain Harry Circle, gave him protection, but a police bureau scandal in 1924 and the violence of the 1926 roadhouse robbery brought an end to Lowe's career.

The 1924 case began with a car accident. On October 9, 1924, Zula Lowe, the bootlegger's wife, traveling twice the speed limit, smashed into another car in the intersection of Northeast Multnomah and Thirteenth Avenue. All four occupants of the other car were injured, twenty-one-year-old Mrs. Magnus Morud seriously. Mrs. Lowe's car wrapped itself around a telephone pole, but she was not hurt. Witnesses said that Zula Lowe was "maudlin drunk" at the scene, and she admitted to motorcycle officer Wiles, who was first on the scene, that she had been drinking. Mrs. Morud was unconscious when she reached St. Vincent's Hospital, and doctors in the emergency room confirmed that the bootlegger's wife was drunk.

Then a strange thing happened. Two doctors went into a "secret conference" with an unidentified policeman. When they came out, they announced that Mrs. Lowe had not been drunk and that she would only be charged with reckless driving. Zula, still noticeably drunk, was transferred to the Central Precinct, where her husband had been huddling with Captain Circle and Lieutenant Frank Ervin, who headed the traffic division. Ervin booked Mrs. Lowe for reckless driving and released her on $250 bail. About a week later, Mrs. Morud, who never regained consciousness, died, and Mrs. Lowe's charges were upgraded to involuntary manslaughter.

The scandal came about because of the actions of Captain Circle. Harry Circle, who joined the police bureau in 1903 and would serve on the force until the early 1950s, had been involved in helping protect criminals in the north end for more than twenty years at the time of the Lowe case. He had been charged with corruption multiple times but never convicted. After a meeting behind closed doors with John Lowe, Captain Circle approached Ervin about Mrs. Lowe's bail, claiming that she should be released on her own recognizance. Ervin, who was deeply involved with protecting the Pullman porters' ring, saw a chance to get a little revenge on a rival and refused to reduce bail. A shouting match between Circle and Ervin ensued, but Ervin would not give in, and John Lowe finally paid the bail in cash and took his wife home. Circle was charged with using abusive language and conduct unbecoming of an officer. He was suspended for ten days without pay and lost his position as leader of the day watch; he was reassigned to

St. Johns, already the usual dumping place for disgraced officers. After this experience, Circle cleaned up his act and served the rest of his career with distinction, involved with the Police Disciplinary Board and helping found the Sunshine Division, which provided financial help and groceries to the poor.

As far as the city was concerned, Harry Circle's crime was not trying to protect a criminal but trying to protect the wrong criminal. By 1924, crime in the city had been well organized under the leadership of Bobby Evans, whose real name was Augustine Ardiss. Evans, a former boxer and matchmaker of the Portland Boxing Commission, was one of the least public members of the "city hall crowd." Losing his position as matchmaker in 1921 after criminal charges for the theft of a diamond ring, Evans had wandered, promoting boxing matches in New York, Denver and San Francisco, before quietly returning to Portland in 1923 and opening the Shamrock Club on Southwest Second Avenue. The Shamrock was a combination boxing gym/cigar store that was a haven for gambling and served as the headquarters for the powerful organization Evans created. A close friend of Mayor Baker, Evans used his connections to bring order to Portland's underworld,

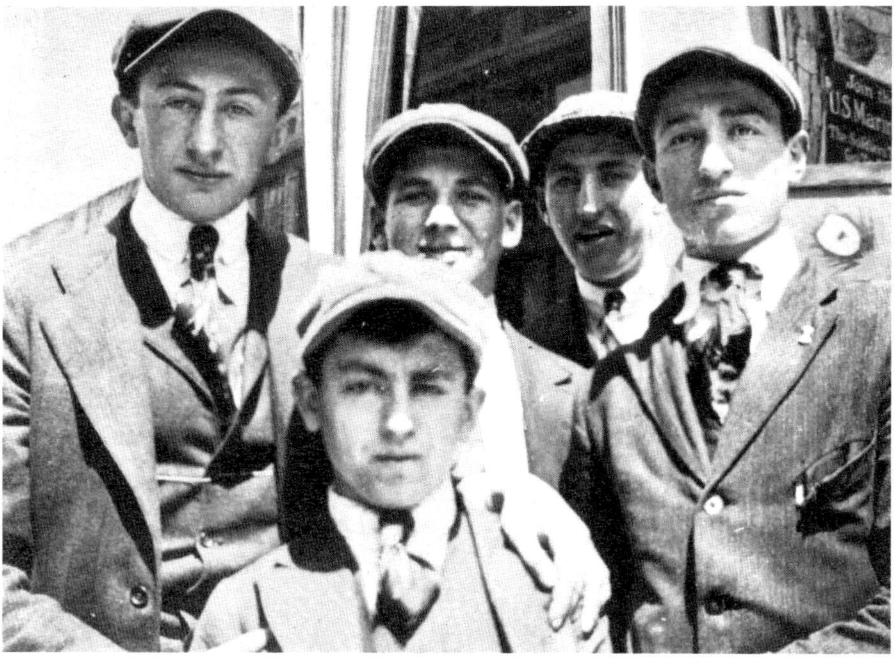

Abe Weinstein (left) and his friends boxed and played basketball at Neighborhood House in South Portland. Bobby Evans recruited Abe and many others as muscle for his criminal operations. *Stephen Weinstein Collection.*

collecting payoffs from Frank Kodat; Royden Enloe, Portland's slot machine king; Roy Moore; and many others.

Royden Enloe had been an employee of S. Morton Cohn, Portland's first slot-machine king. Cohn introduced coin-in-the-slot machines to Portland in the 1890s and invented the coin-operated shoe-shiner in 1904. In the early years of the twentieth century, he expanded his business into real estate development and needed to spin off his semi-illegal slot machine business under the leadership of Enloe. The slot-machine gambling device, known as a "one-armed bandit," was invented in San Francisco in 1892 and introduced into Portland a short time later. By 1899, the city had begun its long battle against the popular device. Cohn used many strategies to make it seem that the slot machine was not for gambling, first paying off jackpots with cigars. Soon, coin-operated machines sold many goods and services, including shoeshines, and started the long, slow process of becoming legal.

Royden Enloe didn't care about the legality of the business he took over from his boss. He recruited waterfront toughs, often from the Longshore or Sailors' Unions, to serve as muscle and used violence and extortion to build his business. Buying his gambling devices from Al Capone's outfit in Chicago, Enloe may have been the first Portlander to have close dealings with the East Coast mob. Enloe not only used Capone's machines, but he also imported the crime boss's violent business model to the Rose City, running a protection racket and expanding his vending machine business through extortion. During the 1922 Waterfront Strike, Enloe pioneered the business of "labor slugging": hiring out his muscle as "goons" to attack picket lines and help break the strike.

In order to exert authority over violent criminals like Frank Kodat and Royden Enloe, Bobby Evans needed some strong muscle of his own. The police department under Chief Jenkins could help, and it was very effective at keeping competition out of town, but it had to keep a clean reputation as much as possible. Evans needed enforcers that he could personally control. He found an excellent source of young toughs in one of his old South Portland haunts: Neighborhood House. Neighborhood House was a settlement house along the lines of the organization Jane Addams had pioneered in the immigrant neighborhoods of Chicago. It provided education and services to immigrants, serving as a community center for both Jewish and Italian families. South Portland, largely destroyed in the 1960s to make way for the Auditorium Urban Renewal Project, was near the old shipyards and became a convenient home for Portland's poorest workers, most of them immigrants from Russia, Italy and Greece. Children of the

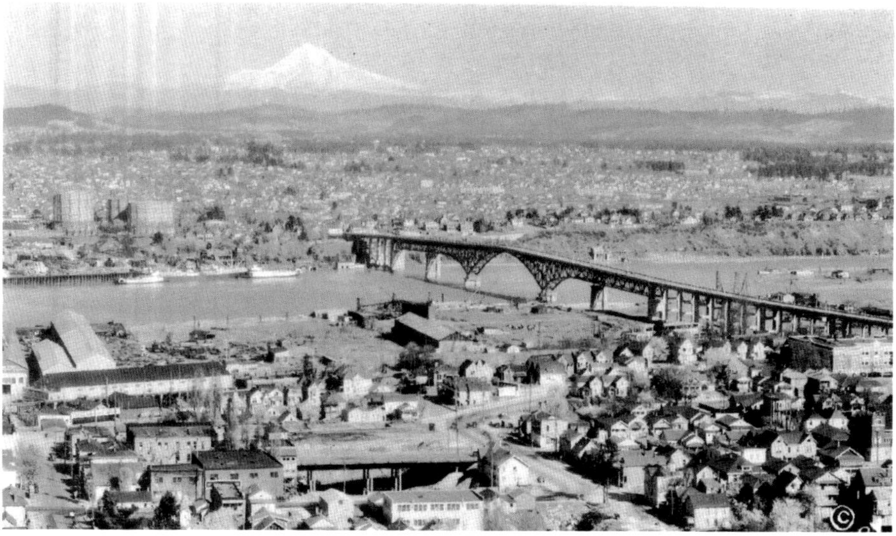

South Portland was the crowded home of most of Portland's Jewish and Italian immigrants in the 1920s. Young men who helped support their families by selling newspapers on the street were prime candidates for criminal careers. *Portland City Archive.*

South Portland neighborhood, especially the boys, quit school early to help support their families by hustling newspapers, shoeshines and other services on the streets. Some of them saw criminal activity as a good source of income.

Neighborhood House created youth athletic programs in an attempt to divert young people from lives of crime, but its programs were easily subverted by Bobby Evans and his friends. Evans, who remained very active as a fight promoter, spent time at Neighborhood House, coaching young boxers and recruiting young athletes for his organization. Many young men, such as Abe Weinstein, Nick DePinto and Jake Minsky made their first contacts with the criminal enterprises that would provide their careers while participating in Neighborhood House athletic programs. Abe Weinstein, one of the most precocious of Portland's young gangsters, was arrested for the first time at the age of sixteen for running a South Portland gambling club.

The 1920s have been interpreted as a time of unprecedented prosperity in the United States, and to some extent that is true. The prosperity people experienced, though, depended more on where they started on the economic ladder and what connections they had with powerful people. While those at the top of the economic heap enjoyed unprecedented prosperity, for most working people, the 1920s were a time of intense poverty. Real estate, insurance, stock trading and bootlegging all offered great opportunities and potentially high incomes, but the main supports of Oregon's economy—lumber, agriculture and shipping—were all in decline. The anti-radical campaigns had greatly decreased the power of unions, encouraging employers to cut wages and make unreasonable demands on their employees. For example, after the unsuccessful 1922 Waterfront Strike, in which the power of both the IWW and the International Longshoremen's Association was broken, wages for waterfront workers were cut and the length of work periods was increased. Unemployment was still a problem, and with no "social safety net," many working-class families, especially immigrant families, were forced to live in dire poverty. A makeshift still in the basement and a barrel of "bathtub gin" could make the difference in supporting a family. In South Portland and East Portland, many working-class women operated stills, brewed beer or fermented wine as a method to make ends meet or for their families' use.

Floyd Marsh, the young miner from Arizona who settled in Portland in 1923 and joined the police bureau in 1926, became one of the biggest critics of the policy of enforcing the prohibition laws against Portland's poorest citizens. In his 1976 memoir, *Twenty Years a Soldier of Fortune*, Marsh tells of the struggle that some of the people he arrested had in trying to pay the twenty-five- and fifty-dollar fines imposed for an illegal barrel of wine. Marsh, called the police bureau's "stormy petrel" (the *Oregonian*'s favorite epithet for critics of the city government), explained how the harsh enforcement of liquor laws against the poor provided good cover for the police bureau's illegal activity. Marsh served on the vice squad from 1926 to 1929, when he resigned from the squad in anger over its political use. He headed the vice squad starting in 1927 and also was the commander of Mayor Baker's "secret police."

The secret police were a shadowy force originally employed to collect evidence of illegal drinking in order to establish search warrants for liquor raids. Most of the "secret police agents," more often referred to as private detectives or stool pigeons, were people who were legally compromised. Their identities usually became known only if they failed spectacularly somehow. For example, Johan Fagerlie, better known as Handsome Hans, who became one of the most notorious of the secret police, was an itinerant logger who was arrested in a raid on a North End "blind pig." With a liquor charge held over his head, Fagerlie was easily convinced to turn stool pigeon. Continuing his drinking and carousing in his usual haunts, Handsome Hans provided evidence for dozens of police raids, thousands of dollars in liquor seizures and many years in jail for his underworld "friends." After being badly wounded by "Wee Willie" Smith, one of Portland's most violent bootleggers,

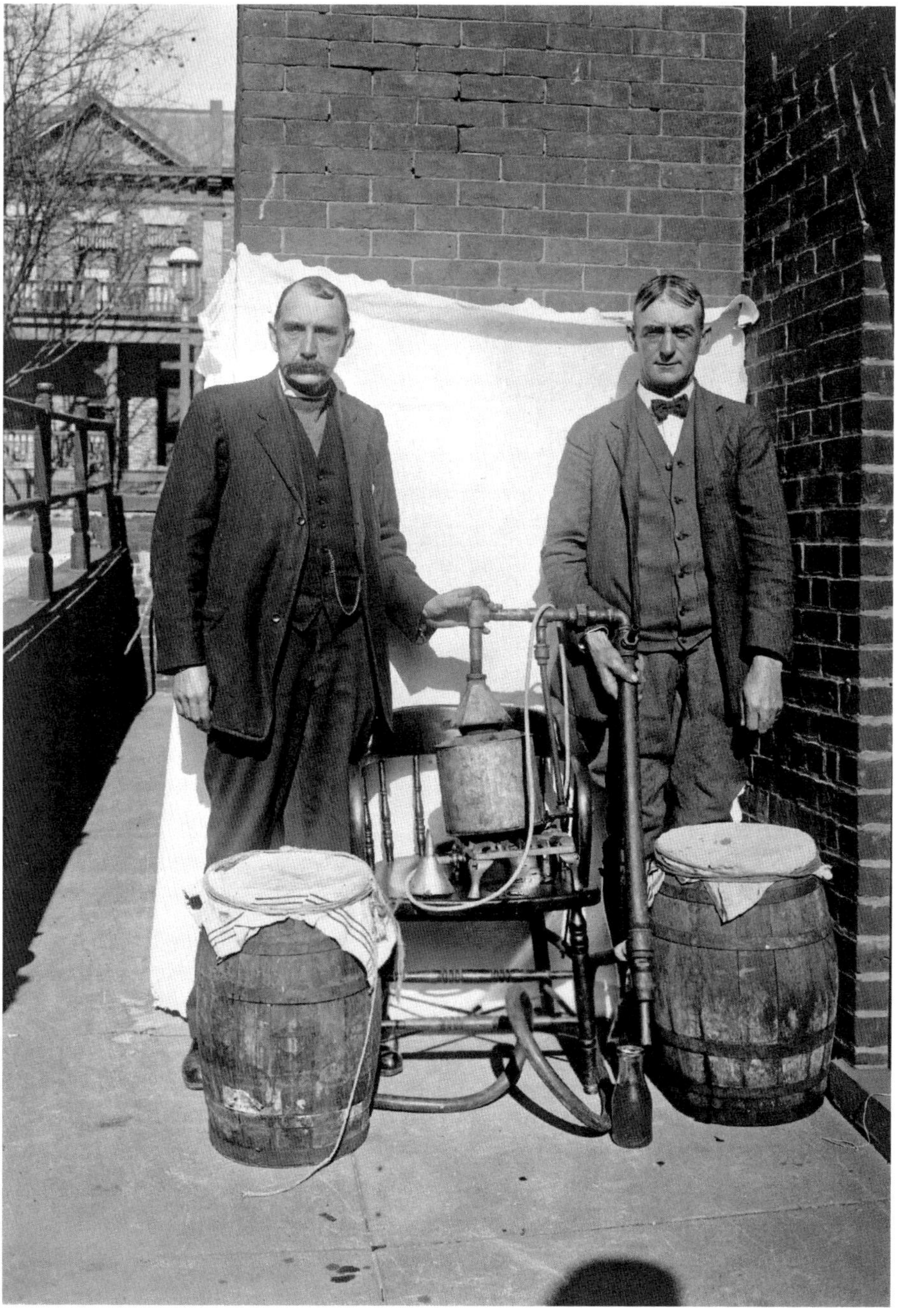

A makeshift still in the basement and a barrel of "bathtub gin" were an easy way to make a living for some of Portland's poorest residents. The police focused their law enforcement efforts on these bootleggers, who were least able to pay the fines they received. *U.S. Library of Congress.*

better known as Smitty the Bootlegger, during an arrest, Fagerlie retired and was eventually awarded a small pension by the city.

Anna Schrader, a woman compromised by a shadowy past and an affair with a police lieutenant, also served as an agent of the secret police. Schrader, a vivacious and attractive woman who was active in both the Republican Party and the Portland Woman's Club, mixed easily in

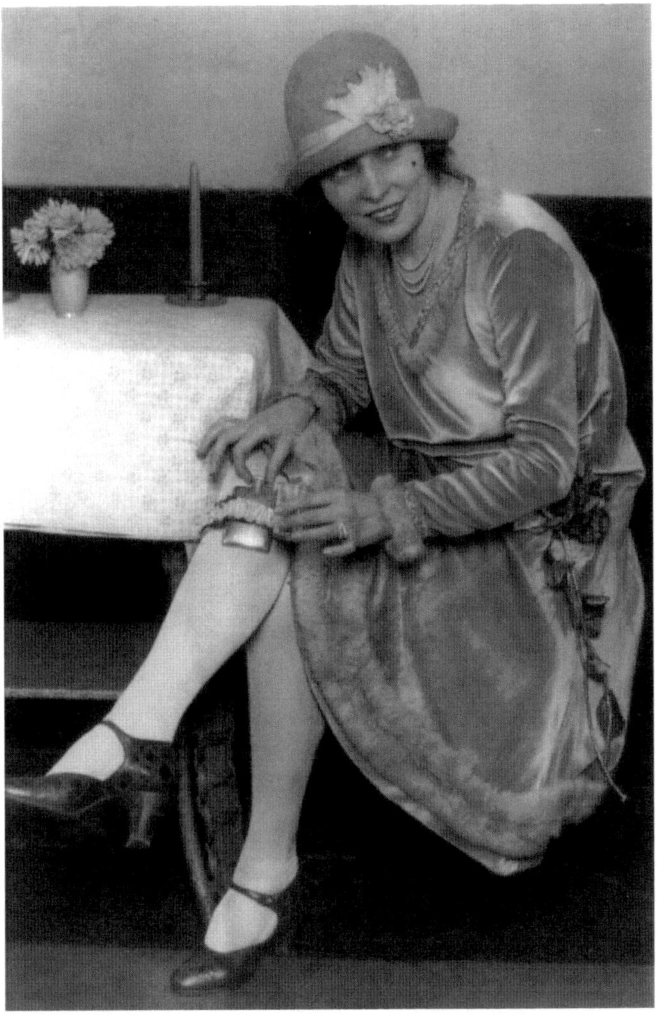

"Dainty Dancer" Mademoiselle Rhea demonstrates the latest fad of garter flasks in 1926. Resistance of the prohibition laws became fashionable as the "lost generation" redefined morality. *U.S. Library of Congress.*

Portland society and kept a close eye on the illegal doings of her set. After the passage of the Volstead Act and the advent of national Prohibition, resistance to the law became fashionable. People of all ages flaunted the law, some drinking openly and publicly with a wink, others hiding their activities in various ways. New laws made possession of alcohol illegal, and public drunkenness remained a crime. Resistance to the law became a cultural norm, and the percentage of people using and abusing alcohol remained high. Prohibition failed horribly in discouraging and suppressing the use of alcohol, but it was wildly successful at increasing the power and the budget of police departments at the local, state and national levels.

In addition to stool pigeons, the secret police had operatives who would "do anything short of murder," according to Floyd Marsh. Marsh named two secret police officers—Roy Cox and John Seeley (probably not real names)—who engineered the "frame up" of Floyd McReynolds, which we will get to in a moment. Black bag jobs (burglaries), blackmail, physical intimidation and smear campaigns were all regular tactics that the Baker administration used against its critics and "enemies," and the secret police were the main arm of this abuse of power. The man affectionately known as "Our George" and the "Kissin' Mayor" was not above relying on his underworld friends to protect his power, and some of them didn't draw the line at murder. For example, Roy Moore was tied up in legal difficulties until 1924 over the Sells-Floto Circus robbery, and in order to make up the economic loss, he seized control of several stills, which he kept moving around the rural areas of Oregon and southwest Washington, supplying much of the lower-grade liquor for markets in Portland and Seattle. To maintain and expand his power, Moore recruited a group of violent men and developed sophisticated techniques to pull off many gangland-style killings. Their technique is best illustrated in the 1945 murder of Joe Mezzina in Portland, in which a troubled World War II veteran took the fall. Not that Mayor Baker had a relationship with Moore in any fashion. That's what Bobby Evans was for.

The McReynolds case is the best documented case of a police frame-up in Portland. Marsh explains exactly how the "frame-up" was accomplished and gives the immediate motive, but he leaves much of the story out of his account. In Marsh's account, the McReynolds case was caused by Frank Ervin's mistake and an effort to save the city from a serious lawsuit. Marsh then absolves Leon Jenkins of any responsibility for his actions, blaming higher-ups in city hall, and goes on to explain how Jenkins abused his power to frame a Portland citizen for a crime. What Marsh leaves out is the bigger context, which becomes apparent only when you know about the background of the people involved. The immediate issue was a liquor delivery that the Union Dollar Cab Company allegedly made in late August 1928. Captain Frank Ervin, head of the traffic division, received a "telephone tip" that Floyd McReynolds, the president of Union Dollar Cab, would be making a delivery of liquor from Sadie Martin's speakeasy, at the corner of Southwest Sixth and Hall Street, on the PSU campus that day. Ervin was very familiar with Martin's place because she participated in the payoff that delivered about $100,000 per month to two "plainclothesmen" who hung around Central Precinct, according to Floyd Marsh. Ervin wasn't interested in raiding Martin's, where McReynolds was picking up the booze, but he was interested in getting McReynolds and closing down the Union Dollar Cab Company.

Union Dollar Cab had been in business only about a year, opened as an employer specifically for members of the Taxidrivers Union. The union had been in a violent struggle with Eddie Tonkin, self-proclaimed "Taxicab King" and crony of Mayor Baker. Tonkin, who shared a "love of cars" with George Baker and founded an auto-dealership dynasty in Portland, was an ex-newsboy and a proud member of the "city hall crowd." A taxi driver and part-time auto race competitor, Tonkin parlayed his relationship with city hall into a manager position with Black & White Cabs and eventual ownership of almost all of the taxis in town. Tonkin gobbled up cab companies by ruthlessly keeping any union activity out of his garages. He employed a "goon squad" of loyal taxi drivers who beat union supporters and denied employment to anyone who showed sympathy for unions. After a disastrous strike in 1928, the struggle became bloody, and it was a regular occurrence for taxi drivers on both sides to be summoned to remote locations where they were beaten and robbed of their cabs.

As Tonkin's power grew, it became difficult for union drivers to find work, and in defense they pooled money to form the cooperative Union Cab Company in 1926. Under the leadership of A. McReynolds, an officer of the Taxidrivers Union, the company declared that all its drivers were men with two or more years' experience, they were members of the union and they would receive a living wage. McReynolds's ne'er-do-well brother, Floyd, opened his own tiny cab company, Union Dollar Cab, a year later. Union Dollar was a tiny operation with two drivers and McReynolds, who acted as dispatcher and back-up driver. Floyd McReynolds was not as idealistic as his union-supporting brother. Union Dollar Cab was used most often to transport liquor and women to illegal rendezvous. The relationship between the two brothers and the "Union" name could both be used to smear the Taxidrivers Union.

Captain Ervin, Chief Jenkins and Officer Marsh may have consoled themselves with the thought that no one deserved to be arrested for bootlegging more than Floyd McReynolds, but the fact is that he was not guilty of the crime he was eventually convicted for. After Ervin received the telephone tip, he and his men swooped down on the offices of Union Dollar Cab. Ervin said they were too late to catch McReynolds in possession of liquor, but they did find a gallon jug of "moonshine" hidden in the garage. With a grin, Ervin pulled the taxi license off the wall and suspended operations of the cab company, pending a city hall review. The license was officially suspended two weeks later, and then disaster struck. The moonshine evidence in McReynolds's case disappeared. No one knows exactly what happened to it, but Marsh makes clear that the evidence room in the basement of Central Precinct was basically the liquor cabinet for the city hall crowd. He gives details of uniformed officers in police cars making deliveries of liquor to city hall and to various other places to turn over to city commissioners and their friends. Wherever the evidence went, it was now impossible to convict McReynolds, and once he had been acquitted, he would have a strong case against the city for pulling his company's license.

According to Marsh, Ervin begged him to use the secret police to get McReynolds, but he refused. It was only after a personal meeting with the chief and Jenkins's smooth, fatherly style of leadership that Marsh finally agreed to arrange for McReynolds's arrest. In his book, Marsh washes his hands of the crime and puts the blame on the pseudonymous Cox and Seeley, describing in detail the elaborate plot that ended with McReynolds's arrest in stunned possession of a gallon of moonshine. His conviction was assured this time, and his lawsuit against the city was a dead letter. Floyd McReynolds was a violent criminal who pimped out his own wife and ran "badger games" against unwary Portland visitors. He participated in the distribution of bootleg liquor on a regular basis. The short jail sentence and fine he received on the false charges were little enough for him to pay, but the illegal and immoral use of the police force was a high price for the city to pay. Floyd Marsh was disgusted with the whole thing and resigned from the vice squad and the secret police in the wake of the McReynolds case. Although he did make an attempt to reform the vice squad when he was briefly reassigned as its leader in 1931 and testified about its practices to the grand jury in 1935, he was never able to make headway. Marsh never received high rank and ended his twenty-year career with the bureau as a patrol officer on the Harbor Patrol.

## CHAPTER 7

# DOUBLE AGENT

## MRS. SCHRADER ROCKS PORTLAND

*I like the men of the police department. They have always been friendly to me.*
*–Anna Schrader*

*Mrs. Anna Schrader, 38, private detective known to many in Portland as an expert swimmer and an ex-candidate for Rose Festival Queen, rushed toward police Lieutenant William H. Breuning pointing a pistol at him, as he drove up to his home at 33 East Church Street. He threw the door open and it hit her hand and caused one explosion, and in the scuffle on the curb, in which the policeman attempted to take the pistol from her, another harmless shot was fired.*
–Oregonian, *August 24, 1929*

"Woman's Bullets Miss Policeman," the headline screamed. It was the beginning of the biggest scandal since the Great War and one of Portland's most lurid sex scandals. Mrs. Schrader was in tears as she sat in her jail cell on the upper stories of the downtown Central Precinct. She said that was not how it happened at all and she had only borrowed the weapon to protect herself because Bill had beat her so badly the last time they were together.

The Schrader/Breuning affair was news for the next couple of years, and the leadership of the police bureau and city hall came under intense scrutiny not only by the public but by law enforcement officials as well. Coming on the heels of Captain Leo Harms's all too public divorce and resignation from the bureau in 1928, police bureau leadership was decimated and morale among officers reached all-time lows. Some officers couldn't help but feel that the police bureau was nothing more than a criminal operation itself, but rising unemployment made them eager to hold on to their jobs at any cost. At less than $100 per week for the average officer, the jobs weren't that well paid either, but it beat the alternative. People forced from their homes because of bank failures and unemployment were already beginning to gather in Sullivan's Gulch in what they sardonically called "Hooverville." In comparison, a small regular salary with the promise of a tiny pension after thirty years seemed all right, especially with the opportunity to earn money on the side.

When Anna Schrader moved to Portland in 1910, running from a past she wanted to forget, she took a room in a northwest Portland rooming house. She wanted to make a mark on the city, and she did. It took a few years to get on her feet, though. In 1915, she married another resident of the rooming house, Edward Schrader, who had a steady job at the Brooklyn Railroad Yard in southeast Portland. Respectably married, Mrs. Schrader became active in the Portland Woman's Club, well known for its puritan and exclusive attitude. She ran for Rose Festival Queen in 1916 as the fire department candidate; she always did like men in uniform. The year 1916 was when she made her mark as a swimmer as well; she was the only swimmer to show up for the annual Christmas Day Polar Bear Club Swim. All alone, Anna Schrader, who had lost an election bet in the November presidential election, swam in the freezing, murky water of the Willamette River.

In 1916, she also met patrolman William Breuning, an ex-miner who had recently joined the police bureau. Breuning was popular among the other officers and sought after for his command of Yiddish, necessary to the officers who patrolled South Portland. The attractive young matron and the dashing young cop liked each other right away. On the witness stand, Breuning would say that he always felt a "brotherly" feeling toward Mrs. Schrader, but it is pretty obvious that they were attracted to each other from the beginning. Although Schrader continued to be an active member of both the Woman's Club and the Multnomah County Republican Party, and she played an active role in all three Liberty Bond drives of the Great War, more and more, her life revolved around her relationship with Breuning. In 1921, she went to work for the mayor's secret police, gathering evidence on illegal drinking for either prosecution or blackmail and participating in "frame-ups" and other dirty tricks. She also began having an affair with Bill Breuning.

The two married lovers kept their affair secret for a time, meeting in Breuning's car, often when he was on duty. As the affair continued, and

Schrader became an accepted member of the police bureau, befriending several officers, the two became bolder, registering under assumed names at several downtown hotels, like the Ansonia and the Cornelius. Sometimes they would meet at Schrader's home when her husband was at work. Years later, when the case became a public spectacle, Anna Schrader described the relationship:

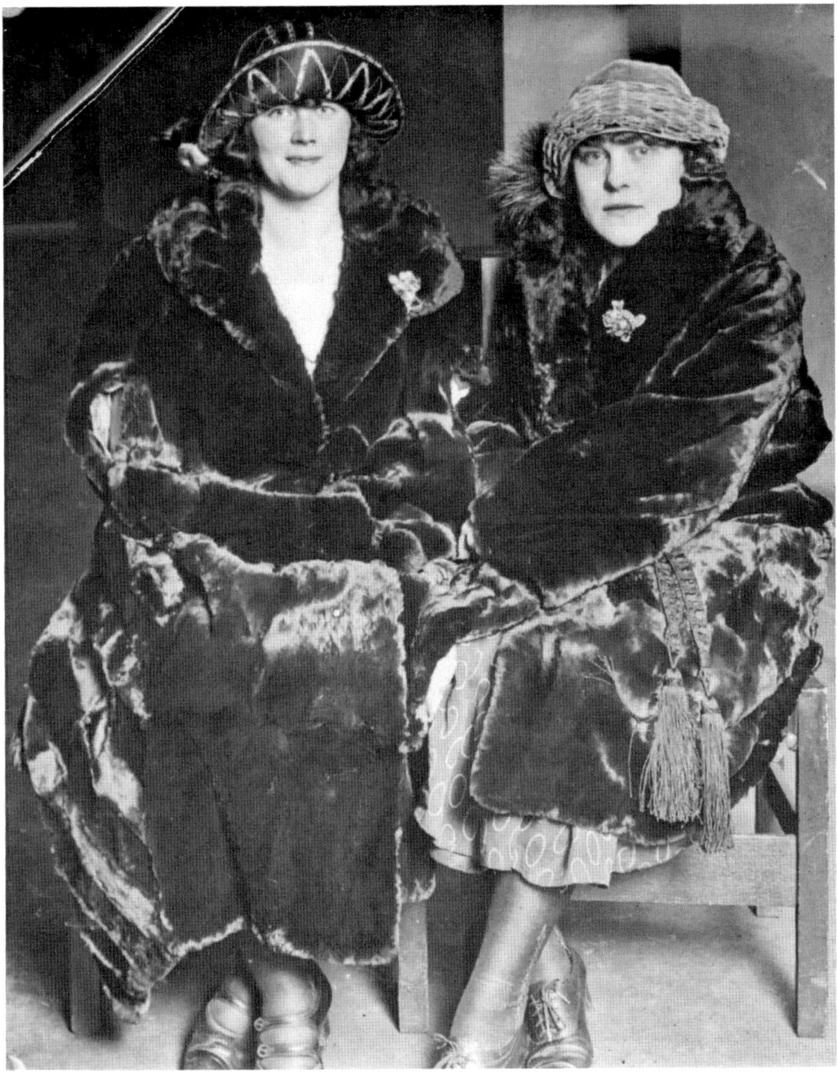

Two women arrested in Portland for drinking in a speakeasy. Their sleek fur coats show that resistance to the prohibition laws transcended class. *Oregon Historical Society.*

> *I have known Lieutenant Breuning for more than fourteen years, but we have been intimate for the past eight...Eight years ago he used to call for me and ask me out to dinner and everywhere. Since then he has hardly missed a night at my house: I know that I have done wrong. He was so nice to me in those early days, saying that he loved me, that I became infatuated with him. Many times he has taken his wife to a show and has come to see me. For weeks at a time he has eaten his evening meals at my house. In all that time, my husband, whom I consider the best man I have ever known, did not know anything about it, for he was working.*

Anna Schrader was a conflicted woman. Trying to forget a past that she wouldn't or couldn't confront, she clung to a vision of the future that was based on fantasy and lack of fulfillment. As hard as she had tried to get Portland's attention in the early days, she tried just as hard to go "undercover" as a private detective for the secret police. Although her police work was partly a cover for the affair with Breuning, Schrader took the job seriously and was well trained. She took great pride in her knowledge of firearms and was especially proud to demonstrate techniques, such as how to disarm a suspect. The evidence she gave on illegal drinking sometimes put friends from her "social set" in jeopardy, so the daily betrayal of "the best man [she had] ever known" was par for the course. With little education and high intelligence, Schrader was prone to flights of imagination and fantasy. These were the things she based her plans on, saying, "Lieutenant Breuning told me repeatedly that he loved me better than anyone else in the world, and that he had bought his wife an automobile so that she might be away in it." Fueled by the romantic tales of Mata Hari (aka Margreet MacLeod), the Dutch exotic dancer and infamous "double agent" of the Great War who was executed by the French in 1917, which was popular in newspapers and film, Anna Schrader lived a fantasy life as a "double agent," both professionally and romantically.

While her husband worked nights, Schrader pretended to be married to Bill, fixing him dinner almost every night. Her neighbors often reported a police car parked on their street for hours, and calls from the public prompted Bill's friends on the force to tell him to park somewhere else. The police bureau was under intense scrutiny as the 1920s came to a close; after a decade of rumor that it was involved in bootlegging, people were starting to notice. One who noticed was Reverend Bjorn Johannsen, a Swedenborgian minister of the social gospel who came from Bath, Maine, in 1928 to take over the pulpit at the New Church in southeast Portland. Johannsen was appalled at the high level of unemployment in Portland and the suffering of many of the city's working people. He was an early strong supporter of the Unemployed Council that was organizing in Portland's working-class neighborhoods. Johannsen was disgusted by the contrast between the poor working people and the city officials who lived lives of luxury and ease.

Disturbed by the fact that Mayor Baker's home mortgage had been paid off by his wealthy supporters, Johannsen was equally disgusted by the waste in the water bureau and the lordly manner of city commissioner John Mann, who ran the bureau as his private domain and drove an expensive Phaeton Sedan. Mann was rumored to have a "private resort" inside the protected area of the Bull Run Watershed, and he ran the bureau like a dictator, dispatching work crews for official jobs and unofficial jobs indiscriminately. Johannsen found an ally in young, left-wing Democratic attorney Harry L. Gross. Founding the Independent Political Forum, Johannsen and Gross began to call attention to the behavior of Commissioner Mann; the sex scandals in the police bureau just gave them fuel.

The 1928 divorce of Leo Harms, with accusations of excessive drinking and multiple adulterous affairs, brought a great deal of embarrassment to

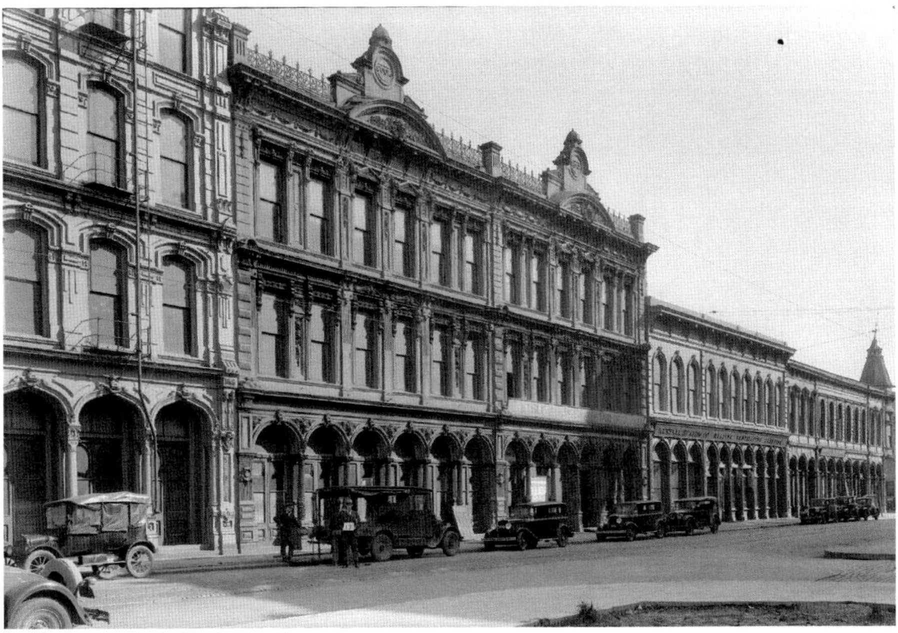

Front Street in 1928 still had much of the look of old "frontier" Portland. These buildings were destroyed for the seawall sewer construction project that spanned several years in the 1920s. *U.S. Library of Congress.*

the city government, especially the police bureau. The bureau's first officer promoted to lieutenant had been the public face of prohibition enforcement in the early days, and the scrutiny the scandal brought to the bureau made the affair that Schrader and Breuning were carrying on dangerous.

Breuning was not willing to give up his loyal and respected wife or their two young children for an illicit relationship that would make him a laughingstock in the intimately connected police community. It was commonplace, at the time, for a powerful married man to have one or more mistresses; it was not commonplace for him to leave his wife for a mistress who would be considered nothing more than a "fallen woman," a party-girl or "chippy." He was not willing to give up his promising career for the fading pleasures of an aging lover, either. As Breuning withdrew and Schrader felt her fantasy world being threatened, she became desperate.

Leading up to the explosive encounter in late August 1929, Anna Schrader was a frustrated woman and had been doing some bad things for a period of time. During one of the most puritanical times in American history, especially harsh on women, Schrader faced serious social pressure and even ostracism when the story of her affair became public. The denials and contradictions regarding that wrongdoing and the double life she was leading began as soon as she was arrested the night she aimed a gun at Lieutenant Breuning. Schrader denied ever trying to intentionally harm him, saying, "It is silly to say that I tried to kill him. I didn't have any intentions of killing him. I carried the revolver because I was afraid of him, and the shells were exploded when he grabbed me and we were wresting over the gun." She declared that while her husband had only recently learned of the affair, he would stand by her and fight for their marriage, believing her when she stated that Breuning had pursued her and had instigated the affair for his own selfish intentions.

She denied ever trying to hurt Breuning when she stated, "Had I wanted to get Breuning I could have done it any number of times. I had only to let my husband come home and catch him, and he could have caught him any one of four times that he came home early from his work in the railroad yards." She said of her husband, "He has known of my affair with Breuning for four months. I told him I had met Breuning in his home and talked to him in the presence of his wife," alluding to the time shortly before she would go public, in which she is alleged to have disclosed the affair to Breuning's wife, Blanche, in Breuning's presence. This disclosure would be the proof Edward Schrader may have wanted, that the longstanding affair was indeed over, and apparently, he was willing to accept it at face value. He loyally stood by

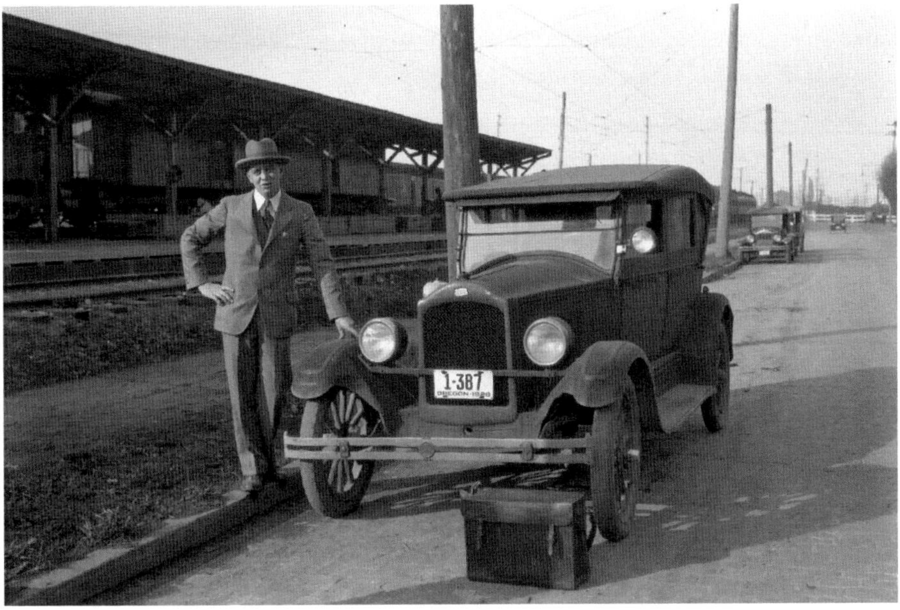

The explosion in auto ownership after the Great War ushered in a mobile society that offered many opportunities for social anonymity. The availability of cars was a boon to some occupations such as traveling salesmen or "drummers." *Portland City Archive.*

his wife during the scandal and claimed that Breuning had "alienated" his wife's affections.

Breuning scheduled a meeting with his wife, Blanche, and Chief Jenkins on August 25, 1929. With Schrader's extensive police connections, she quickly got wind of it. Schrader was desperate to be understood and felt that she was being misrepresented by Bill and everyone else. To learn that there would be a meeting with the chief of police, to which she was not invited, proved too much. She was enraged. "I wanted Chief Jenkins's good opinion," she declared. "They had been trying to put all the blame on me." She had formerly responded well to Chief Jenkins's paternal style and saw him as a father figure, craving his approval.

"Was it hurting your work as a private detective?" an *Oregonian* reporter asked Schrader. "No, that didn't enter into it," she answered, "but it hurt me to think that the chief and others in the department would believe that I had been calling Mrs. Breuning up and talking to her. I never did that. Why should I? He was married and had no intention of obtaining a divorce, and I was married to the best man in the world and had no intention of asking for a divorce." She said the chief had told her and Breuning that they must straighten their affair out between themselves without letting it cause a scandal in the police department.

She was particularly offended at the rumors that Breuning was spreading about her among other police officers. He told everyone he knew that she was crazy and getting out of control. The officers of the police bureau started to become polarized, with some of them supporting Lieutenant Breuning and some of them siding with Schrader. Some of Breuning's partisans went so far as to raid hotels like the Grant and Rector, tearing pages from the register. Schrader was providing details of the affair, including the false names they had registered under, and Breuning was still denying that the affair had ever happened; the unidentified "detectives" were trying to make it impossible to verify Schrader's story. Schrader's emotional style sometimes made her seem crazy, and she may have had an emotional breakdown of some kind—it would explain some of her actions, and this only made it harder for Portland to believe what she had to say. That aspect of the scandal only made her more determined to tell her story and be believed. She filed a suit against the city for false arrest, and her husband filed an "alienation of affection" suit against Breuning. "They may think they can settle this thing out of court with me before the case comes up for trial," she declared. "They can't, though. I wouldn't drop this case for all of John D. Rockefeller's money. We are going to see it through and I am going to tell a lot of things that no one will want told."

Paranoid Anna Schrader may have been, but that didn't mean they weren't out to get her. Shortly after her suit was filed, someone fired a pistol through the front window of her northwest Portland apartment. The police who investigated swept it under the rug, claiming a "potted cactus" had fallen through the window from the balcony above—an absurd claim considering the configuration of the window and the apartment complex. Over the next several months, bricks were thrown through Schrader's windows on multiple occasions. Bricks through the window became a classic form of intimidation of both the Teamsters' Union and the gangsters who infiltrated their union so readily. It was also a tactic used against the auditor who investigated the water bureau's finances in 1929. In addition, Schrader would become the frequent victim of "hit and run" traffic accidents. Her car was smashed up several times, but she was not injured. Captain Frank Ervin, who was boasting about his loyalty to Chief Jenkins in the "bitter battle" they were waging against Schrader and other police bureau enemies, didn't break a sweat investigating the accidents that plagued his enemy. He just ordered his men to give her a parking ticket whenever they saw her car.

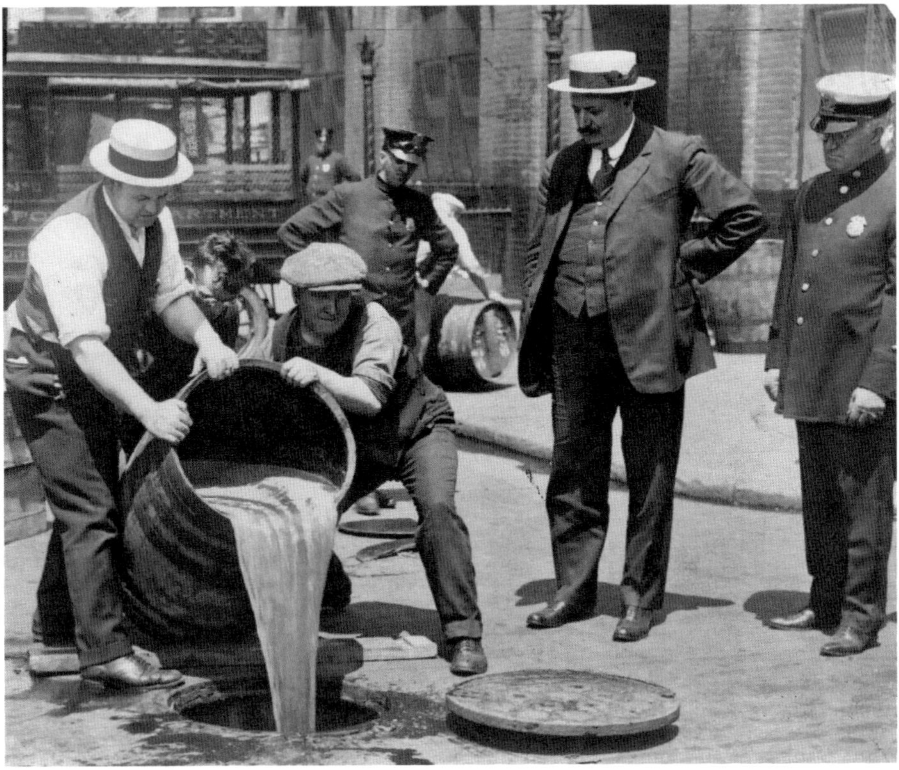

Dumping beer and other liquor into the sewer was a good photo op for local politicians who wanted to court the "dry vote." There was a scandal in 1916 when a secret tap was found in the sewer line at the Multnomah County Courthouse that allowed some unnamed person to recover dumped liquor. *U.S. Library of Congress.*

Schrader was angry at the loss of her job and what she felt was the betrayal of Chief Jenkins and became very vocal in her criticism of the police bureau and the city government. She claimed that she had a "little black book" in which she kept her investigative notes and if that information ever came out it would "rock Portland." In an angry meeting with Mayor Baker, who tried very hard to put the lid back on a scandal that was seriously challenging his power, Schrader exclaimed, "You are not so clean yourself." The mayor, always his most honest when he got angry, shouted, "No, I am not clean, and I don't pretend to be. I hope you don't try to bring me into this case, as I don't believe that you can."

Others believed she could, though. In 1930, Reverend Johannsen and congressional candidate Harry Gross formed the Citizens' Recall Committee and began circulating petitions to recall city commissioner John Mann for malfeasance in office and Mayor Baker for neglect of his duty for doing nothing about the corrupt water bureau that was already in debt more than $1 million. Anna Schrader, angry at the mayor and the chief of police, quickly joined the committee and became one of its most vocal speakers. She did radio broadcasts in favor of recalling the mayor and reforming the police bureau. She also made public appearances, and on at least one occasion she was heckled during a speech and assaulted afterward by three women who kicked her in the shins. One of the women charged with assault in the "shin kicking" case had been arrested at least once in a downtown brothel connected to Bobby Evans's organization. Clearly, it was dangerous to oppose the beloved mayor of Portland.

Schrader didn't back down, enduring public humiliation as she was told to "sit down and shut up" by the judge at one of her many court appearances. At one point, she was forced to act as her own attorney and became bogged down in legal jargon. She confessed to the judge that she had "only a sixth-grade education" and was doing her best. She testified at grand jury meetings investigating the doings of John Mann, Mayor Baker, newly elected city commissioner Earl Riley and even District Attorney Lotus Langley and Chief Jenkins. Mann eventually lost his position and was sentenced to jail for his felonious management of the city water bureau and Mayor Baker came near being recalled from office, but no one else on the mayor's team suffered serious consequences. Schrader continued to pop up any time there was criticism of the police bureau or there was a sex scandal there (as there was again and again). Occasionally, she would even wave around what she claimed to be her "little black book" and threaten to tell all, but she never did.

For some reason, Anna Schrader never agreed to "name names" as she had promised to do so many times, and the elusive "black book" remained closed. The question of why she never revealed the secrets she claimed to have is the great mystery of her life and of the Baker administration. At this date, we'll never know. She said she wouldn't take "Rockefeller's money" to keep quiet, but she might have been frightened into silence. We don't know much of anything about Anna Schrader née Tierney's life before she came to Portland in 1910, but Chief Jenkins, or other members of the police bureau, may have known a great deal. Did they hold something over her head to keep her quiet?

Bill Breuning's promising career was ruined by the 1929 scandal. First suspended without pay for thirty days, Breuning was fired for "conduct unbecoming an officer" when he returned to work. The chief needed to make an example of Breuning to take the heat off of the bureau, and

Breuning's conduct in lying and trying to cover up the affair gave him a good excuse. Breuning's wife and two children stayed with him, but they couldn't have been a very happy family. With unemployment rising in northeast Portland where they lived, Breuning had a tough time finding a job. Finally, after the United States entered the Second World War in 1941, Breuning was hired, along with several men who had been fired from the bureau, as a "special officer" assigned to patrolling retail neighborhoods at night. Paid by local merchants, the specials were armed and endowed with police power but not sworn members of the police bureau. This system has been controversial throughout Portland's history but used frequently at times of high crime or during wartime. However you look at it, Breuning's professional life was ruined, and he probably held a deep grudge against his ex-lover, Anna Schrader.

## CHAPTER 8

# THE GEORGE BAKER FOLLIES

*The Constitution of the United States specifically provides that a person shall be innocent until he is proved guilty. An indictment by the Grand Jury is nothing more than an accusation subject to be tried before a court.*
*—George Baker*

On August 1, 1921, some of Portland's most important civic and law enforcement leaders began to gather in a room at the Multnomah Hotel for a mysterious meeting. Mayor George Baker, police chief Leon Jenkins, Sheriff Thomas Hurlburt, District Attorney Lester Humphries and several others had received mysterious messages summoning them to the meeting. All of the participants said they had no idea who had summoned them or what the meeting was about, but all of them were there. As the men stood around helping themselves to refreshments, a photographer was getting ready to snap a picture. Pretty soon, he had all of the city leaders grouped in front of a large velvet curtain, posing for a picture. Just before he snapped the picture, freezing the moment in time, two figures dressed in white robes and pointed white masked hoods stepped out from behind the curtain. The picture, which ran in the next day's *Portland Telegram*, shows the leaders of the city, some with shocked expressions on their faces, standing in a group with two Ku Klux Klan members in full regalia. The headline over the photo read, "Chief Kluxers Tell Law Enforcement Officers Just What Mystic Organization Proposes to Do in City of Portland."

It was a brilliant move for the fledgling KKK, implying that it already had power and influence over the city's leaders. There was some truth to the implication, too, since it had managed to gather them all together for a meeting that they claimed they knew nothing about. In the picture, Chief Jenkins looks more surprised than anyone, and it is not a stretch to think that he was angry about the prank. Jenkins never liked the KKK and spoke out against it several times, but the organization became very popular among members of the police bureau. By 1923, it was estimated that half the members of the force were also Klansmen. The organization kept its membership rolls secret, so it can be difficult to determine who was and who was not a member, but it is clear that it had huge popular support in 1922 and 1923. Luther Powell, king kleagle of Oregon (the main organizer), and Fred Gifford, exalted cyclops of Portland (a local leader), the two hooded Klansmen in the photo, were taking a chance and going public with their organizing campaign. The gamble worked.

Luther Powell, who had already successfully organized klaverns—KKK chapters—in Medford, Roseburg and Klamath Falls, came to Portland to replace an organizer who had gotten on the bad side of the national organization. Powell quietly got the word out and built a hard-core cadre of Klansmen to help him, appointing Fred Gifford, a popular local electrician, as exalted cyclops—leader of the local klavern. By the summer of 1921, when the infamous photo was taken, Powell and Gifford were ready to begin an organizing drive that would recruit thousands of members to the "secret" organization and see the Oregon KKK reach the highest political attainments the Klan would reach in the country.

Many historians have taken George Baker's presence in the photo as evidence that he was a member of the KKK. Baker was a joiner, and it would have been in character for him to join the Klan—he rarely passed up a social invitation. Baker courted the KKK vote in his 1924 run for the Senate and his run for reelection as mayor that year as well, but the truth is he never joined the Klan. According to Lem Dever, a traveling journalist from Tennessee who settled in Portland in the early 1920s and edited the KKK organ the *Western American* before splitting with the Klan in 1925, claimed that he and many other Klan members doubted Baker's "racial qualifications" for membership. According to Dever, Baker never asked to join the organization, and he wouldn't have been allowed to if he had. The truth was that Baker didn't need to join the Klan. According to Dever, Exalted Cyclops Gifford had the goods on "Our George." Dever says, in his 1925 exposé *Masks Off!: Confessions of an Imperial Klansman*, that Gifford

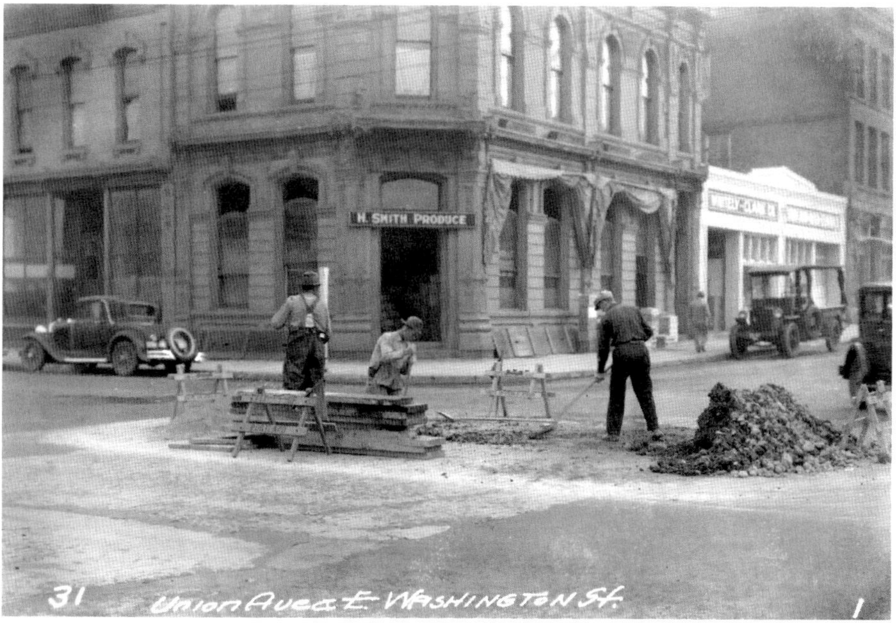


The rapid growth of Portland after the Great War made construction a lucrative business. Infrastructure improvement projects were the main way the city relieved serious problems of unemployment. The projects were all riddled with graft, corruption and kickbacks. *Portland City Archive.*

had evidence that could send Baker to jail for years and used to brag about keeping that evidence in his desk and the fact that he could wrap Baker around his little finger.

We don't know what evidence Gifford had on Baker, but there was a lot that it could have been. He may have had information on the dirty election tricks pulled by the *Oregonian* in Baker's favor in 1917. He probably knew about the police bureau's involvement with bootlegging on the mayor's authority. He might have had evidence linking Baker to the mysterious death of his ex-wife in Washington State in 1919. He might have known about the insurance kickback scheme that Baker and his stepson, Brace Galloway, were involved in. Baker had many crimes hidden away in his closet. Whatever Gifford knew, it was enough to make Baker do the Klan's will—for a while.

George Baker's administration was touched by scandal repeatedly during the sixteen years he served as mayor—beginning with charges of campaign finance irregularities during the 1917 election and charges of immorality at the 1918 Oregon Auto Dealers' Convention. Baker was cleared of alleged crimes in both cases by a grand jury in March 1918, but rumors of corruption, graft and other crimes persisted. Baker's administration was an "old boys'" network of men who worked and socialized together and saw little boundary between the two. Important decisions were usually made based on the social and financial concerns of Portland's leading businessmen and other members of the "city hall crowd." As E. Kimbark MacColl pointed out, while there is no evidence that George Baker ever personally gained from graft and corruption, his friends did.

His family did, too, but there were certainly problems within the mayor's family. Divorced in 1909, a scandalous development at that time, the first Mrs. Baker, Bertha Elinor Blair, a registered nurse, moved to Seattle and remarried. In 1919, she drowned in an apparent accident in her second husband's boat. Her husband, Walter Miller, a former King County deputy sheriff and professional photographer, was arrested after the accident, and police considered charging him with murder. Brace Galloway, Baker's stepson, also died mysteriously and after his death was implicated in another scandal. Galloway graduated from Hill Military Academy in 1920 and went to work for Harvey Wells and Company Insurance. He was a valuable young insurance agent since he brought most of the city's automobile and property insurance with him. The cozy relationship between the Wells Company and the city came to light in 1924 in the wake of the County Bridge Scandal (which we'll get to in a moment). The insurance deals associated with the bridge deal were very similar to what the mayor was doing with the Wells Company. It became an issue during Baker's reelection run for his third term in 1924, but it was not enough to keep him from being reelected. By the time the insurance deals came to light, Brace Galloway was long dead. He was shot to death at the age of nineteen in 1921 in the living room of his stepfather's home on Southeast Twenty-eighth Avenue. It was an accident—two young hunters fooling around with a new rifle when it discharged. Baker's family had some hard luck.

Luther Powell didn't hesitate after the infamous picture ran in the *Telegram*; he began to hold public recruiting meetings at Civic Auditorium, with the mayor's blessing. A series of talks, entitled "The Truth About the Invisible Empire" and sometimes featuring the motion picture *The Face at Your Window* (1920), a drama about the supposed danger that immigrants pose to American jobs, brought in thousands of members. At one meeting, 1,200 new members were initiated at once. Cinema was an important tool for the KKK revival that took place in the 1920s. The post–Civil War terrorist association, the original KKK, was glorified in the D.W. Griffith film *Birth of a Nation* (1914). Although cinematically innovative and creatively brilliant, the film is a vile polemic of hatefulness and is considered to be the most important influence on the rebirth of the Ku Klux Klan. By 1923, the Klan had organized in nearly every state in the nation, even those with no historical foundation for it, like Oregon. Not that Oregon was free of racial prejudice—far from it. Anti-Chinese organizations that worked openly in Portland in the 1870s and 1880s were every bit as deadly as the Ku Klux Klan, but there were very few African Americans in Portland at that time—fewer than 1,000, with the population growing to around 1,500 by 1920. Klan hatred had to focus on other groups: Asian Americans, Catholics and union supporters. With the historical basis in anti-Asian hatred and the influx of Catholic immigrants from southern and eastern Europe, the Klan found fertile ground in Portland.

Beatrice Morrow Cannady, founding secretary of Portland's National Association for the Advancement of Colored People (NAACP), protested unsuccessfully against the presentation of *Birth of a Nation* in 1915 and 1918. Cannady argued that the film was "libelous to the Negro race" and that it would aggravate the racial situation in Portland. Both times, the film had extended runs and was seen by enthusiastic crowds of white people. In 1922, when John Hamrick scheduled the film for presentation at his Blue Mouse Theater as part of the Ku Klux Klan organizing drive, the NAACP protested again. Hamrick showed his support for, and probable membership in, the KKK by advertising himself as 100 percent John Hamrick—a direct reference to the KKK's "100 percent American" slogan. Incidents of KKK-inspired violence in Medford, Roseburg, Oregon City and Portland had upped the stakes considerably. At Cannady's urging, James Weldon Johnson, national president of the NAACP, wrote to Governor Ben Olcott, stating, "In the interest of law and order we urge you that you prohibit this exhibition." Olcott, still complacent about the threat the KKK posed, failed to act, and George Baker was not inclined to act, either. The film opened at the Blue Mouse on April 1, 1922, advertised as the "8th Wonder of the World." It played to enthusiastic crowds, and KKK membership soared.

By the end of 1922, Oregon was estimated to have more than fifty thousand KKK members, most of them in Portland. Regular cross burnings were held on Mount Tabor, and Mount Scott had a "perpetual" fiery cross visible. Large "klavalcades"—automobile parades with hooded KKK members—drove through the streets of southeast Portland; Klansmen shouted slogans and urged people to join the "invisible empire." The growing numbers of KKK membership translated to power at the polls. The Klan backed candidates in local and statewide races in 1922 and backed the

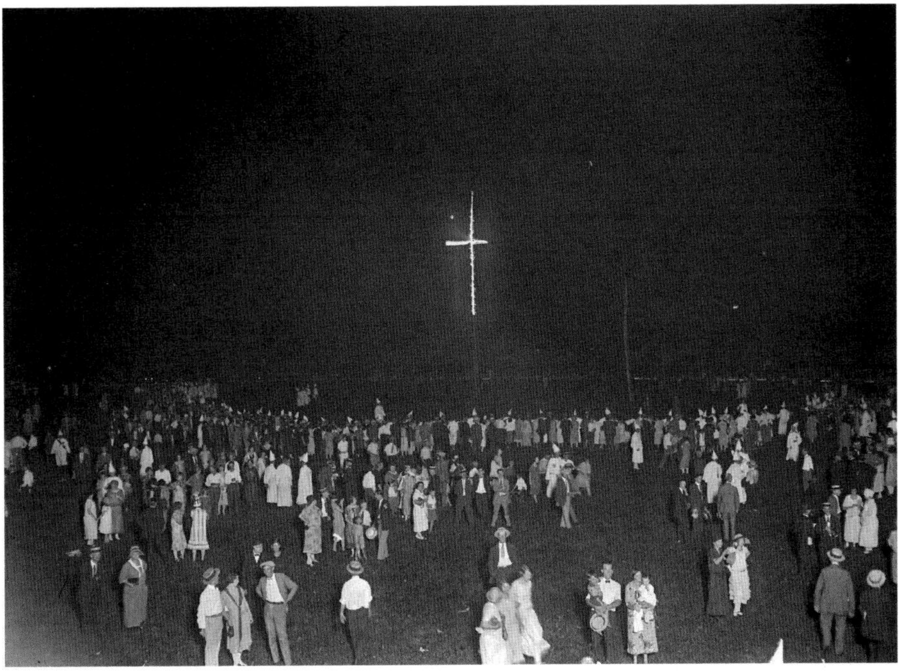

As KKK membership grew in Portland, the Invisible Empire started holding regular cross burnings on Mount Tabor and Mount Scott. Parades of hooded Klan members in cars drove through the streets with loud slogans to encourage others to join. *Portland City Archive.*

"Compulsory Education" initiative on the ballot that year. Complacent governor Ben Olcott lost his job, replaced by the KKK-backed Democrat Walter Pierce. The Compulsory Education initiative, a thinly disguised attack on Catholic schools, passed but was ruled unconstitutional by the Supreme Court before it could take effect. Locally, the Klan elected many members to the state legislature and senate, including K.K. Kubli, father of the Syndicalism Act, who became president of the senate. In addition, Klan support was important in electing two members of the three-man Multnomah County Commission: Dow Walker and John Rankin.

The Klan presented itself as in support of "law and order," and many of its members were police officers or members of the one-hundred-man Police Vigilantes. It has been reported that all of the members of the Vigilantes, which later became the Police Reserve, and about half of the police force were members of the KKK. There was a large crossover of membership between the KKK and the American Legion (AL), a veterans' group made up of veterans of the Great War. The AL "assisted" the police frequently and often participated in violence against union supporters and immigrants, especially Japanese. It is clear that the KKK's commitment to "law and order" was hypocritical. For example, a group of "Police Vigilantes" was fired for impersonating Portland police in order to seize a shipment of liquor from bootleggers, which they kept for themselves. In Medford, the Jackson County sheriff was charged with collusion in a plot to kidnap and whip three black men. In Oregon City, there was another near lynching, and in Marshfield (Coos Bay), Timothy Prentiss, a Great War veteran and active member of the African American community, was castrated and murdered in 1924. The Coos County sheriff immediately left town after the murder, and the AL "assisted" the police in their investigation. Although Marshfield's tiny black community offered a reward of $500 for the arrest of the killer, no one was ever charged with the murder. In Portland, Elise Reynolds, the wife of a Union Depot porter, was beaten, and a K was burned into her cheek with acid. A note left at the scene, signed KKK, warned the Reynolds family and all other blacks to stay out of the northeast Portland neighborhood where they had recently moved.

The KKK denied any involvement in acts of violence. In the Reynolds case, they claimed that someone was trying to frame the Klan for the crime by leaving the note and burning the K into the woman's cheek. It was typical for the Klan to try to blatantly intimidate communities, and it wouldn't be unusual at all for the Klan to leave such obvious clues. With nearly thirty thousand Klan members in Portland, many of them involved with the police bureau, the terrorists had little to fear and could operate as openly as they wanted. KKK-backed political candidates were elected to office in campaigns that promised to reform the corrupt system that was in place, but those claims were just as hypocritical as the claims that they were nonviolent.

The hypocrisy became undeniable in 1924 during the so-called Bridge Scandal. Corruption, graft and kickbacks were standard practices on municipal construction projects since the earliest days of the city. Mayor Baker's terms in office only facilitated such activity, but Dow Walker and John Rankin, both KKK-backed candidates for the Multnomah County Commission, campaigned against such practices and promised to reform the county's operations where construction was concerned. Rankin and Walker, a close friend of Mayor Baker and former manager of the Multnomah Athletic Club, were both overwhelmingly elected and joined Chairman Charles Rudeen on the commission. On the same ballot, Portlanders had approved a $5 million bond issue to replace the Burnside Bridge and to build other bridges to help relieve growing traffic congestion.

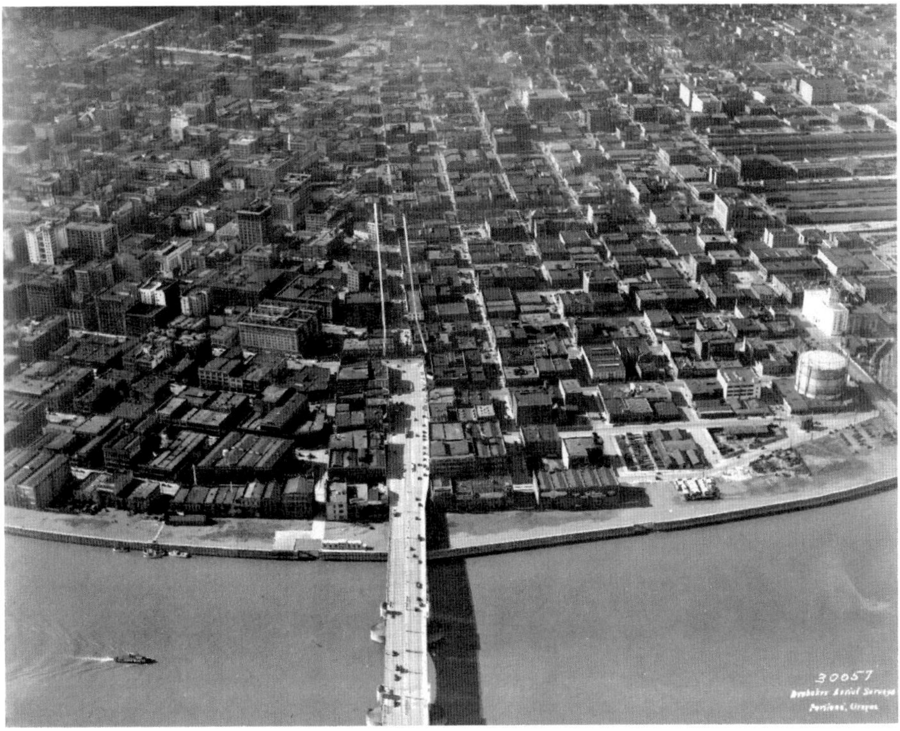


The seawall and sewer project lasted for many years and completely transformed Portland's waterfront. The new Burnside Bridge (pictured) opened in 1926 and was the center of a huge scandal that humiliated the KKK in 1924. *Portland City Archive.*

The Burnside Bridge, built in the 1890s with substandard materials, was already becoming unstable, and traffic was often restricted because of the bridge's safety. The new county commission made plans to replace it as soon as possible and also made plans for the Ross Island Bridge, to connect South Portland with southeast Portland, and the Sellwood Bridge, at the southern edge of Multnomah County. On April 1, 1924, Multnomah County opened bidding for the bridge project for only twenty-four hours. In the short window, the county received two bids: one was a three-bridge deal; the other was just for the Burnside Bridge. The commissioners, who were surprised that the second bid came in, closed the bidding window quickly. They approved the three-bridge deal, even though the Burnside Bridge portion was $500,000 higher than the second bid. C.F. Swigert, president of the Pacific Bridge Company, who had submitted the lower bid, sued the county. Within days, the new governor, Walter Pierce, ordered an investigation that uncovered some uncomfortable facts. For example, Dow Walker, an insurance agent, handled all of the insurance for the contractors and received high commissions for the transactions. The three commissioners split a $50,000 cash payoff between them after awarding the contract. Chairman Rudeen and Commissioner Rankin were discovered to own property on the east side of the Willamette that they sold to the county at a high price, after spending more than $500,000 to change the location of the bridge so that it would require their property. Much later, historian E. Kimbark MacColl uncovered the fact that during the deal Walker had acquired several lots on the east side of the Burnside Bridge at extremely low prices; these properties, not discovered at the time of his trial, allowed the disgraced politician to retire in style.

Within days, the City Club of Portland issued a report, concluding that "the County Commissioners have forfeited the confidence of the public." Recall petitions began to circulate immediately, and all three commissioners were recalled in May. They also faced criminal charges, but all three were acquitted on technical issues. The scandal, usually referred to as the "Rotten Bridge Deal," disgraced the KKK as a political entity. Other financial misdeeds doomed the organization in Oregon. The high initiation fee of $10 ($130 in 2015) was rumored to be the main goal of KKK organizers, who lived lavish lifestyles using the initiation fees they collected. As soon as the organization had a few members in Portland, it opened an office in the Pittock Block and announced plans to build a ten-story building downtown. Although funds were raised to construct the building, nothing else was ever done on the project, and newly initiated Klansmen felt they had been cheated. Luther Powell Klavern #1 was losing members by the end of 1924, and by 1925 it was pretty much a dead letter in Portland. The American Legion continued to do its hateful work for decades, though. The Ku Klux Klan was gone as an organization, but the hatred remained. After the Second World War, the KKK revived in Oregon, and the problem persisted for the rest of the century, at least.

The Ku Klux Klan was not unique in its participation in graft. Baker's "scratch my back, I'll scratch yours" approach to government encouraged it. Although graft and corruption were familiar elements of Portland's government since the earliest times, they reached new heights during Baker's reign. Street paving and municipal construction, garbage collection, insurance, concessions at civic events, even office supplies in the city hall were all subject to kickbacks, bribery and favoritism—in the form of "sweetheart deals" and "no-bid contracts." Charges of corruption and graft against the mayor and various city commissioners were common. George Baker was subjected to grand jury investigations several times and faced recall elections on more than one occasion. In 1921, the *Oregon Voter* uncovered the fact that Franklin Griffith of Portland Power and Light and several other wealthy supporters of the mayor paid off a $7,100 mortgage on Baker's southeast Portland home. Griffith had heard that Baker was considering stepping down as mayor after only one term because he was not making enough money. This is one episode that contradicts Kimbark MacColl's assertion that Baker never personally profited from graft during his administration. Baker's personal charm and popularity, as well as personal relationships with judges and other influential people, protected the mayor every time.

It was not just in city government that graft and corruption flourished. Unethical behavior was involved in the failure of many Portland businesses during Mayor Baker's terms: Wilcox Investment Company, Pacific Grain Company and the Ladd and Tilton Bank to name a few. Three dramatic business failures and trials over the winter of 1927–28 not only shook the economy, but they also kicked off the Great Depression in Portland much earlier than it hit the rest of the country. The first scandal, involving the Bank of Kenton, actually began in December 1926 with the arrest of bank president J.V. Burke, who was indicted with five others on charges of fraud and embezzlement. The bank had been forced to close its doors when an examiner found a deficit of over $300,000. Burke had made several fake deposits into the account of United Meat Company, of which he was vice-president. Many accountholders in the Kenton neighborhood lost their savings, but John Ainsworth of the U.S. National Bank guaranteed the deposits, averting a panic. Ainsworth and his wealthy friends were not as successful when it came to the case of the Northwestern National Bank.

J.V. Burke served on the board of directors of the Columbia Country Club with Emery Olmstead and J.O. Elrod, both of whom had similar financial scandals in their businesses. Olmstead was the president of Northwestern National Bank. Northwestern was built on money from the lumber business, and John Wheeler, president of the Trask Timber Company and owner of the *Portland Telegram*, was one their major customers. Wheeler, who claimed to come from a wealthy family in Pennsylvania, was actually in an extremely shaky financial condition by 1926. He and Emory Olmstead came up with a plan that historian E. Kimbark MacColl referred to as a "massive check kiting operation." When a bank examiner discovered an $800,000 deficit that had been covered up by fraudulent bookkeeping, he refused to let the bank open its doors on February 28, 1927. John Ainsworth advanced $1 million to keep the bank's doors open, but by the middle of March, the bank was found to be short by over $2 million, and word was spreading quietly that there was serious trouble. On March 28, there was a run on the bank, with depositors lining up on the street to demand their money. Further investigation showed that bank president Emory Olmstead had approved nearly $5 million in bad loans and overdrafts. Olmstead was indicted for fraud, and the U.S. National and First National Banks guaranteed over $2 million in deposits to avert the crisis. Many wealthy Portlanders lost their savings, including the Henry Pittock estate, which lost over $2 million.

Two weeks after Olmstead and Wheeler went on trial, another business failure shocked Portland. The collapse of the Overbeck and Cooke stock brokerage, although nowhere near the loss of the Northwestern National, shook Portland even more. Hundreds of investors lost a total of over $1.5 million in one of the most destructive scandals of the 1920s. During the stock market craze of the mid-'20s, Overbeck and Cooke became a symbol of the "hot" economy and the quick riches that seemed available to any bold investor. When it became apparent that James Cooke, one of the firm's senior partners, was looting investor accounts in order to maintain a lifestyle that included expensive cars, wild parties and outrageous liquor bills, Overbeck and Cooke became a symbol of the greed and corruption that seemed endemic in the "roaring" '20s.

Unethical business practices were not the only cause of the Great Depression. There were several other factors as well: falling prices for lumber and agricultural products; the closure of the shipyards after the Great War, which put more than thirty thousand people out of work (unemployment remained a serious problem through the 1920s); the failure of unions in the 1922 Waterfront Strike, among others, which encouraged employers to cut wages—to name just a few. Faith in capitalism and the economic theories of the Republican Party were badly shaken. Worsening economic conditions inspired working people and the unemployed to turn to the Communist Party for help. Soon, Unemployed Councils, providing direct action support and political education, were organized in Portland neighborhoods. Many of the organizers were ex-Wobblies, but they came from all kinds of backgrounds. For example, Lem Dever, the former KKK writer, was an organizer for the Unemployed Council in the 1930s.

Faith in the law was shaken, too. Revelations about the police bureau, exposed by the Schrader-Bruening Scandal, not only hurt police morale but also tainted the public perception of the police bureau and severely hurt public confidence in the police. More and more people were coming to understand that the prohibition laws were enforced selectively and that they didn't stop drinking or the social problems that came with it. The laws only seemed to encourage drinking and illegal behavior. Even worse, prohibition seemed to encourage corruption and graft in government and law breaking by the police. A popular "repeal" movement sprang up in opposition to prohibition. The movement would finally be successful in 1933, when the Eighteenth Amendment was repealed and intoxicating liquor became legal again.

The world was a different place in 1932 than it had been in 1922. The writing was on the wall for prohibition, and the bootleggers were looking for new opportunities to keep obscene profits rolling in. Gambling and prostitution seemed to be areas of growth, and Bobby Evans saw those pursuits as the best way to keep his empire afloat. After the incarceration of Roy Moore, his organization was absorbed into what became known as the "Joe Brown Ring." Nicholas Tingas (aka Joseph Brown) was the leader of the ring that took over the large still used by Roy Moore. Brown's attorney, Walter Tooze, was very adept at retrieving seized evidence; in fact, he retrieved the same still at least three times. Tooze, who was acquitted of bootlegging conspiracy charges in 1931 (not the first time he faced serious legal charges), later became a Multnomah County judge. More than thirty people were indicted in the conspiracy that supplied Portland, Tacoma and Seattle with moonshine for about five years. In 1932, Tingas went to federal prison, and Bobby Evans was left as the major bootlegger in Portland.

The lack of organized competition combined with cooperation from the police inspired Bobby Evans to expand his empire. At this late date, it is difficult to say exactly what motivated Evans's power grab in 1932, but it is easy to see that greed and overconfidence were part of it, as well as a little political revenge. By that time, Evans had built a strong organization loyal to him personally and under his control. Nick, Ray and Mike DePinto, three Italian brothers who provided muscle for Evans's brothels and protection racket; Abe and Hyman Weinstein, brothers with an interest in burglary and fencing; and Jake Minsky, a taxi driver who served as a "vice caterer," were all from South Portland, part of Evans's gang and participated in his grab for power.

It began with the Seawall Public Market project. Since 1926, Mayor Baker and his friends had made plans to build a new public market building on the riverfront between the Hawthorne and Morrison Bridges. As part of the controversial seawall/sewer project, which completely changed the face of Portland's waterfront, Front Street property owners had been promised a waterfront Public Market that would increase their property values. A new Public Market was needed because of the run-down, crowded conditions

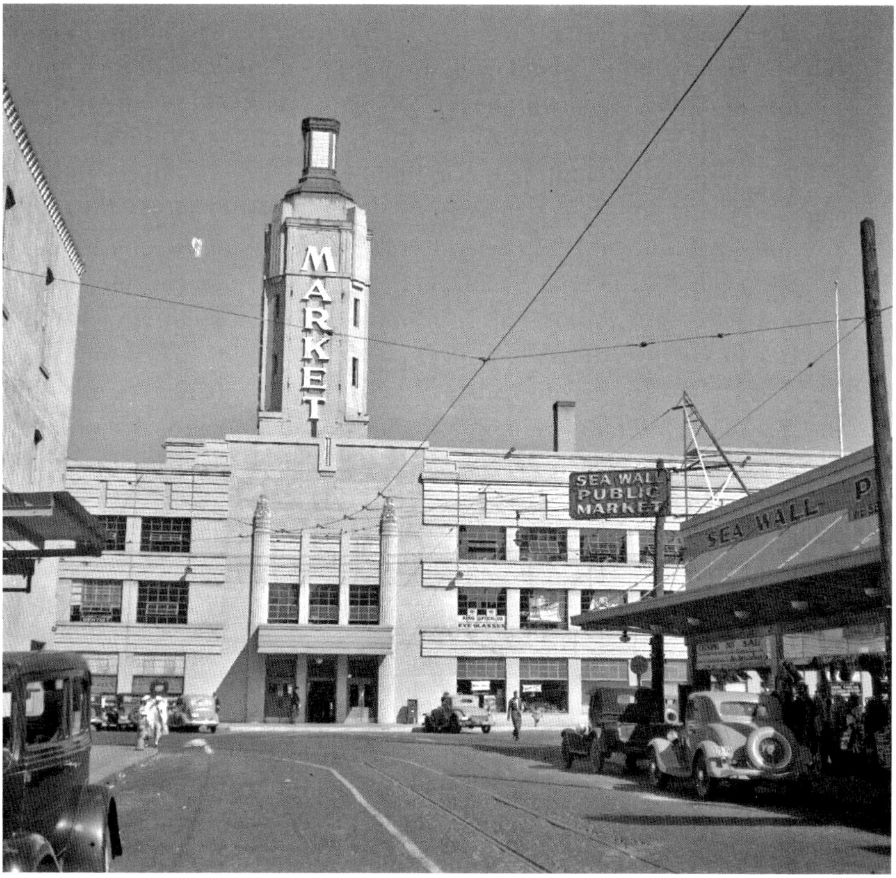


The Public Market Scandal was the last straw for most Portlanders. Mayor Baker survived the recall election narrowly and decided not to run for a fifth term as mayor. Photograph by Arthur Rothstein. *Portland City Archive.*

of the Yamhill Public Market near the corner of Southwest Third Avenue. Plans went forward for the new market, but financing problems and public opposition delayed the project. By 1931, the public had changed its mind about the market, seeing the large construction project as a way to put hundreds of unemployed people to work. The original financing plans were scrapped, and a new application was made to the Reconstruction Finance Corporation, a federal agency that provided funding for relief projects. The Public Market project was back on track.

The location was up in the air, though. Mayor Baker and Governor Julius Meier favored the waterfront site; others promoted a site at Southwest Fifth and Yamhill Street—a location much closer to the retail shopping district.

Eventually, the city council settled on the waterfront site, which was partially owned by Governor Meier. The council agreed to buy the property for the site, spending more than $480,000 for property assessed at $200,000. Revelations about city commissioner John Mann's abuses of authority were starting to come out in the press as a grand jury prepared indictments for the councilman; trust of the city government reached an all-time low in the last year of Baker's administration. Soon, the mayor himself was under investigation by a grand jury for bribery in the Public Market deal.

The *Oregonian*, which still heartily supported Baker years after his friend Henry Pittock's death, claimed that the bribery charges against Baker were an attempt to scare him away from the run for Congress he was contemplating. In several heavy-handed editorials, the newspaper flayed the "Committee of Fifty" that organized a recall campaign against the mayor. The committee, chaired by Reverend Bjorn Johannsen of the New Church (Swedenborgian) and with Harry L. Gross, a leading labor attorney and perpetual political candidate, as its main spokesman, refused to release the names of the "fifty" for fear of retaliation, but they gathered more than seventeen thousand signatures in support of the recall of Mayor Baker and Commissioner Mann. The recall of Commissioner Earl Riley and District Attorney Lotus Langley did not qualify for the ballot because not enough signatures were certified. A special recall election was scheduled for May 20, 1932.

Bjorn Johannsen and Harry Gross had been involved with the grand jury investigation that finally indicted John Mann for malfeasance in office. The charges against Mann mostly centered on his conduct as utilities commissioner: he charged his expensive automobile to the water bureau and routinely assigned water bureau employees to construction projects on his "private ranch" inside the Bull Run water reserve. In November 1931, the new district attorney Lotus Langley, who had been elected with Johannsen's support the year before, decided there was not enough evidence to indict Mann, and the case was dropped. By that time, allegations had arisen that Mayor Baker, Mann and Earl Riley had all accepted bribes to choose the waterfront location for the market. Johannsen and his attorney Harry Gross set up the Committee of Fifty to recall not only Mann but also Baker, Riley and Lotus Langley. One of the most bitter election battles in Portland history ensued.

In January, Johannsen was forced out of his position as pastor of the New Church; several of the parishioners organized a recall of their own for a pastor they felt was too political. Johannsen continued to preach, eventually founding a new Swedenborgian church. He also continued his political activity. Charges of soliciting a bribe were made against Harry Gross, who

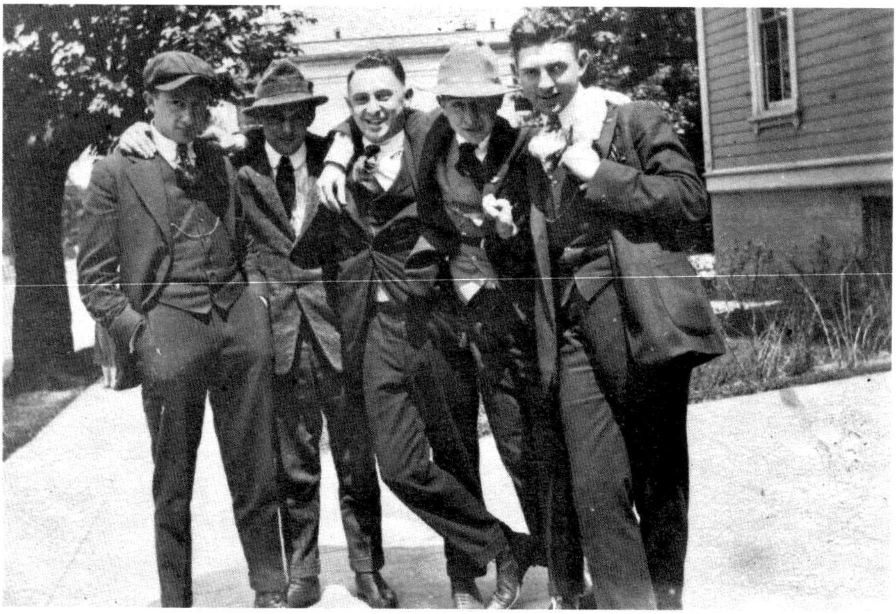

Abe Weinstein (left) and buddies on the street. Weinstein was sixteen when this photo was taken and already running a gambling club in South Portland. *Stephen Weinstein Collection.*

was a stockholder in a company that was proposing that the Public Market be located on Southwest Fifth and Yamhill Street. Mayor Baker claimed that Gross came to Seaside, where the mayor was weekending, and offered him $10,000 to choose the alternate site. It is interesting that the bribe that Mayor Baker claimed he turned down exactly mirrored the bribe he was under indictment for accepting. Mayor Baker came out swinging when the recall campaign got started, claiming that the Committee of Fifty was really a bunch of gangsters and racketeers and that's why they wouldn't reveal their names. The *Oregonian* ridiculed the committee, referring to Johannsen as "kingfish" of the "secret committee."

There was good reason for opponents of the mayor to keep their names secret, though. Besides social pressure that ousted Johannsen from his job, his family was harassed by threatening phone calls and burglaries. Armed men were seen lurking on the street in front of Johannsen's Southeast Pine Street home, threatening his family. Mayor Baker's accusations of gangsters and racketeers exactly mirrored the activities of his good friend Bobby Evans. And the violence was only increasing.

Gangster films hadn't come to Portland yet, but Spencer Tracy had been a big hit at the Oriental Theater in *Dr. Jekyll and Mr. Hyde* in January. His bestial performance could have set the pattern for Bobby Evans in 1932. Beginning with the dynamiting of a gambling club on Southwest Tenth and Washington Street on March 23, Nick, Mike and Ray DePinto unleashed a crime wave that the *Oregonian* called a "reign of terror." A series of robberies began to hit gambling parlors and blind pigs that didn't conform to Evans's will. On April 21, the office of the Committee of Fifty in the Davis Building was burglarized; petitions bearing as many as 1,500 signatures in support of recalling the mayor were stolen. The police bureau and the *Oregonian* seemed to be mystified over who would want to steal the petitions, but the motive became clear when the newspaper announced that the recall had not gathered enough signatures to recall any of the targets.

City auditor George Funk eventually had to agree that it was not legal to impose a deadline on a recall petition, and two days later, enough signatures were certified to have a ballot on both Baker and Mann. The burglary was not completely successful, but it did protect District Attorney Langley, who would be the lead prosecutor when the gang was finally arrested. On June 9, less than two weeks after Mayor Baker's triumphant, but narrow, victory in the recall election, the DePintos dynamited the front porch of Reverend Johannsen's home; the reverend's wife and two children were home at the time of the bombing and narrowly escaped injury. Another bombing hit a gambling den on Southwest Ankeny Street on July 21. Bobby Evans's name was first mentioned in the case later in July when his employee Frank Lavodie was shot five times in the legs during a dispute with Nick DePinto.

Lavodie may have been having an affair with DePinto's wife, but the personal argument brought the DePintos and Evans under scrutiny. After the August 29 bombing of the Fair Hotel, a well-known brothel where more than twenty-five arrests had been made since 1925, and the arrest of Abe and Hyman Weinstein, the whole conspiracy started to come out. In September, it was reported that Evans admitted being behind the whole crime wave, but he later denied it and was acquitted by a jury before the end of the year. The mayor was acquitted of malfeasance in the Market Scandal just days before the recall election and ended his career on a note of triumph, although his decision not to run for Congress or reelection was a retreat. The era of George Baker was over, and Portland was not the same city it had been.

# CHAPTER 9
# HATCHET JOB
## THE MURDER OF FRANK AKIN

*No form of law violation is, or will be, countenanced by me.*
*—Mayor Joseph Carson*

It was a little after 8:00 a.m. on November 20, 1933, when Imo Akin said goodbye to her husband, Frank, who was still in the bath, and left their apartment in southwest Portland for her job as a teacher at Shattuck School. Frank Akin, a forensic accountant who had been conducting an investigation of the Port of Portland for Governor Julius Meier, continued dressing and was just about ready to leave the apartment when there was a knock at the door. Akin was expecting a cleaning lady, so he didn't follow his usual routine; he left his loaded handgun in a nearby desk drawer and didn't engage the chain lock he had installed on the front door a few months earlier. Earlier in March, Akin had answered a knock at his door only to be met by a man with a drawn pistol. "Stick 'em up," said the gunman, but Akin had punched the armed man in the face and then slammed the door, foiling the attack. According to his wife, after the March attack Frank had installed the chain lock and always had the pistol in his hand when he opened the door. Because of the cleaning lady's expected arrival, he didn't follow his new habit.

Akin must have been angry to be confronted by another man with a gun when he opened the door, but this time the gunman had the drop on him. Instead of fighting, Akin backed into the living room with his hands raised. He may have been trying to reach his handgun as the killer stepped into the apartment and closed the door. The killer kept his pistol pointed at Akin and fired one shot that hit the investigator in the right eye. The killer may have searched through Akin's papers and possibly took some that were related to his recently completed investigation of the Port of Portland or the new investigation he was just starting on the city water bureau. It was never clearly determined what was missing from Akin's apartment, but the killer had been paid to eliminate Frank Akin, and that's what he did. Less than two minutes after the shooting, the killer was gone.

Potentially, there were some witnesses who may have seen the killer. Marie McFarlane, a neighbor who also lived in the Arbor Court Apartments, saw a tall, thin man in a long coat and wearing a hat standing on the corner across the street from the apartment building a couple of evenings before the murder. Jean Hendricks, a young mother who lived in the building, said she saw a man in a gray overcoat and hat standing on the steps of the building as she left at about 8:30 a.m. He seemed to be looking for his keys, and she let him in as she and her four-year-old son, Jackie, walked toward his kindergarten class. Glenn Powell, the janitor, was sweeping the steps that morning but didn't see anyone.

Mrs. G.E. King, who lived in the apartment downstairs from Akin, was awakened by the gunshot and also heard the body fall to the floor. She didn't think anything unusual was going on, and Akin's body wasn't discovered until a few minutes later, when the building's super let a cleaning woman into Akin's apartment. It might seem strange that a woman, hearing a gunshot and a body fall to the floor in the upstairs apartment, didn't even call the police, but Portland was a pretty lawless town in 1933, and Mrs. King had heard violence at the Arbor Court Apartments before. Besides the "attempted holdup" of Akin in March, there had been a major police raid at the building in April in which four armed robbers were captured. The large building in the quiet neighborhood near Southwest Jefferson and Fourteenth Avenue was not as safe as it appeared, but then neither was Portland since Mayor Baker had left office at the beginning of the year.

The new mayor, Joseph Carson, probably didn't know about the tight relationship that Baker had with Bobby Evans and the control that the city was able to exert over the town's criminal element because of that relationship. The payoff and the wide-open crime continued, but now it was no longer under the city's control. The new police chief, Burton K. Lawson, Carson's military commander during the Great War and a law enforcement officer with his own ethics problems, was considered an outsider by the rank and file police, and chief inspector Jenkins, demoted from chief, had a disproportionate influence over the bureau. Jenkins's control had slipped,

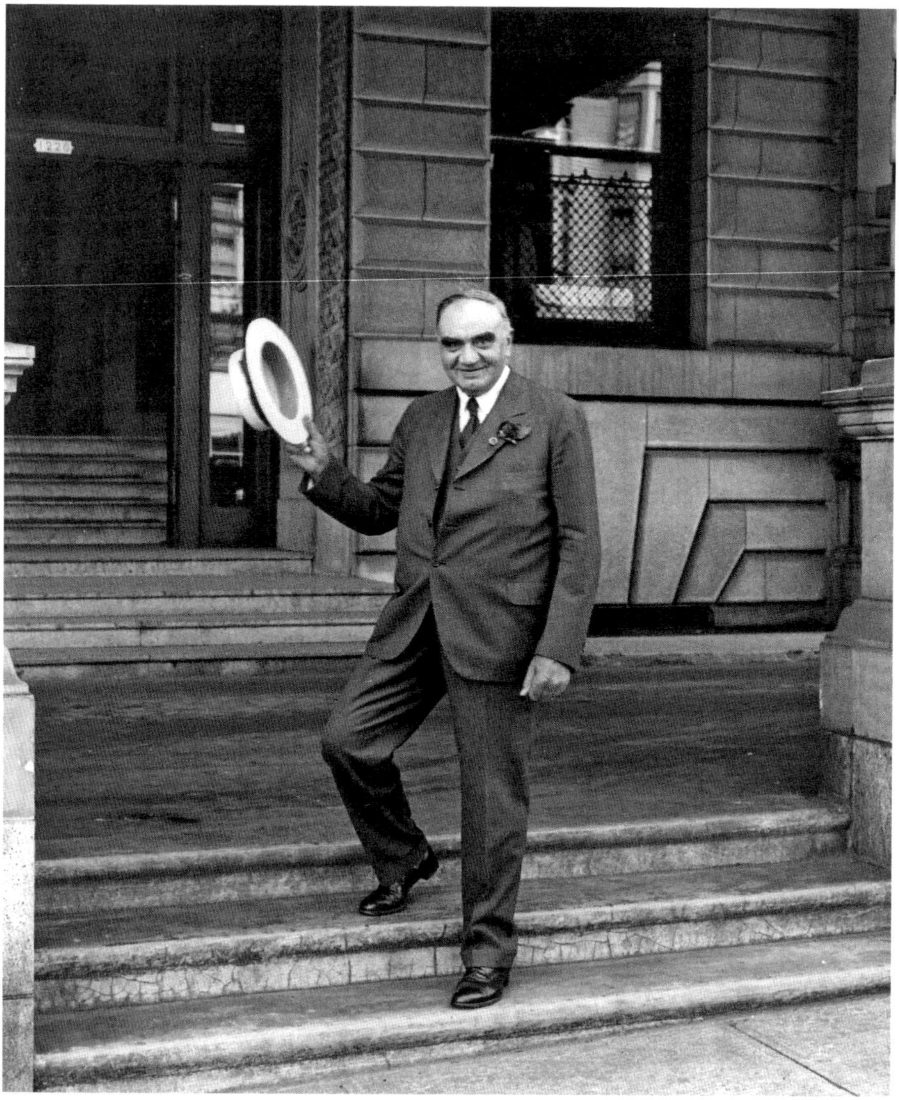

After serving four full terms, "Our George" Baker stepped down as mayor in January 1933. The passing of Baker's strong administration left a power vacuum on both sides of the law, and the 1930s saw a struggle for control of both the police bureau and organized crime. *Portland City Archive.*

too, though, and the bureau was riven by factions, each trying to exert control over its own domain. The power of the Red Squad grew considerably under the leadership of Lieutenant Walter Odale, but the morals squad was weakened by scandal, internal problems and legal alcohol.

Local bootleggers were looking for new opportunities as the illegal liquor trade slowly passed from the scene. The strict controls of the Oregon Liquor Control Commission and the high taxes imposed on liquor in the aftermath of prohibition continued to create a demand for illegal liquor, and some, like Tom Johnson and his Pullman porters' ring, continued to smuggle alcohol into the city. Johnson would continue to derive a steady income from tax-free booze for the next twenty years, but he was already starting to expand his interests into real estate and entertainment. Since 1919, housing segregation, although not official or legal, had been strictly enforced, forcing African American Portlanders to concentrate in the neighborhood stretching north from the Broadway Bridge into the old Albina neighborhood. Williams Avenue was the main street of Darktown, as it was often called, but it would be another decade before it became the vital center of music and nightlife it was later known for. In the 1930s, Johnson was quietly buying up property in the neighborhood and consolidating his power there. Some of the clubs along Williams Avenue were already starting to get a reputation for after-hours jam sessions. Headliners like Louis Armstrong, Duke Ellington and Billie Holiday would perform for segregated audiences at Jantzen Beach and other venues, but after the show, they would head for jam sessions on Williams Avenue, where they played for mostly black, integrated crowds. The integration of audiences on Williams Avenue would be a problem for the white power structure and later would be the focus of efforts to close down clubs in the neighborhood, such as the Dude Ranch.

Bobby Evans, greedy for power, had overreached by backing the violence of the DePinto brothers and the recall ballot scandal. Although he was still a powerful figure in organized crime and ran wide-open gambling parlors in several locations downtown, he no longer had control of the city. Al Winter, a young lawyer, sportsman and friend of Louis Dragna of the Los Angeles crime family, controlled the Transcontinental Wire Service in Portland, which provided horse race results for all of the off-track betting parlors that paid. Control of the wire service put much of the power in Winter's hands, and he would steadily build on that until, by the end of the 1930s, he was far more powerful than Evans had ever been. Embarrassed by the terrible publicity of 1932, Evans would keep a fairly low profile for the next forty years, but he would remain a factor in organized crime, gambling and sports in Portland well into the 1970s.

Roy Moore was back out of jail, but his liquor business was gone, and many of his enforcers were in jail on various charges. The early 1930s were a tough time for Moore, and he served a short term in the Oregon State Prison for petty robbery. On the questionnaire he filled out upon entering prison, Moore wrote that the reason he robbed a store in Coos Bay was because he was "broke." It would be a while before he got his career back in shape, and then it would be based on armed robbery and contract murder rather than liquor. Frank Kodat continued to operate, but the 1933 Walker-McLain double murder brought unwanted attention to his organization. Everyone knew what Shy Frank was really doing, and it was not rehabilitation. His "no jobs in Portland" rule kept him safe, and he continued to organize robberies all over the Pacific Northwest until he finally went to jail again, federal this time, in 1940. Royden Enloe had a large and prosperous coin-machine business, with slot machines, pinball machines and jukeboxes in most of the taverns, restaurants and small stores in three counties. While building his empire, Enloe had become addicted to alcohol. Drunkenness and marital problems took a serious toll on his life over the next few years, making him vulnerable when petty thief Jim Elkins came to town in 1937 and took over his business.

Another crime boss came on the scene in 1931, when Walter Banaster (aka Little Dutch Herman) was pardoned by Julius Meier, the newly elected governor. Banaster, known as Bannister after his pardon, was the only surviving member of the trio who robbed the Claremont Roadhouse on the highway between Portland and Linnton in 1919. Although the robbery of the popular roadhouse had netted nearly $3,000 for the robbers, rumors still circulated that the "robbery" had really been a cover for the murders of Jasper Burgess, a member of the state highway commission, and George Perringer, a prominent rancher from Pendleton. Perringer and Burgess, on a junket to Portland, were drinking with some women from the Benson Hotel when the robbers burst through the doors with guns drawn. The robbers went straight to Perringer's table and shot both men to death before robbing the rest of the guests. Umatilla County's "heroic cowboy sheriff," Tilman D. "Til" Taylor, a personal friend of both victims, came to Portland to help the police catch the killers, but he and newly appointed police chief Leon Jenkins were very careful to deny rumors that the men had been killed on purpose. They maintained that it was just a robbery and nothing more. Taylor's death in a jailbreak just one year later and the establishment of Hyman Weinstein, brother of Abe and loyal member of Bobby Evans's organization, as the "vice lord" of eastern Oregon still raise questions.

Banaster's accomplices, James Ogle and Dave Smith, both conveniently died in prison, and though both of them insisted that Banaster had started the shooting at the Claremont, he was not blamed for the violence of the robbery. Pardoned in December 1931, Banaster immediately returned to Portland and went back to work. In July 1933, he was arrested with two other men. They all had weapons and burglar tools on them and were suspected of several jobs going back to 1932. The case against Banaster (Bannister) was dropped within days, but he probably felt that Portland was a little hot. He moved to Olympia, Washington, about one hundred miles north of Portland, and set up a "resort" known as the Wigwam. Olympia, midway between Portland and Seattle, provided a good base for operations in both cities, and Banaster continued to plan and execute robberies in both states. There is evidence that he had a "murder-for-hire" racket as well, dispatching paid killers for hits as needed.

Julius Meier, scion of the Meier and Frank Department Store family and now governor, had been involved with the Portland payoff for many years before he moved to Salem. As a prominent attorney and activist in the Republican Party, Meier had inherited Henry Corbett's role as the liaison between the party and the city government. All through the 1920s, Meier received a cut of the $175,000 monthly payoff that members of the city government received from organized crime. The payoffs were made through Tommy Luke, a close friend of Mayor Baker and a popular florist. A society wedding couldn't really be of the highest class without flowers by Tommy. According to Phil Stanford's sources, Luke gave a monthly envelope to Meier with his cut in cash. If Meier followed Corbett's habit, as there is little doubt he did, he used the money to advance the interests of the Multnomah County Republican Party. Accusations of vote buying, payoffs, slush funds and dirty tricks had been a regular and disregarded criticism of the powerful political party. By 1933, Meier had been in Salem for two years and had little connection or control over the situation in Portland. The struggle for the Port of Portland Commission is a good example of how Meier tried to reestablish his power in Portland.

The Port Commission of Portland was established in 1891 as a supervising authority for the municipal dry dock and to oversee dredging operations in the shipping channel between Portland and Astoria. Historian Barney Blalock gives an excellent account of the history of dredging this channel in his book *Portland's Lost Waterfront* (2011). Heavy silt flowing down the Columbia blocked the channel on a regular basis, making navigation impossible in some spots. When it was blocked, oceangoing vessels were forced to remain at Astoria while cargo was "wharfed" up and down the river, greatly adding to expenses. Keeping the Columbia-Willamette channel dredged to a minimum of twenty-five feet was vital to the city. Starting in

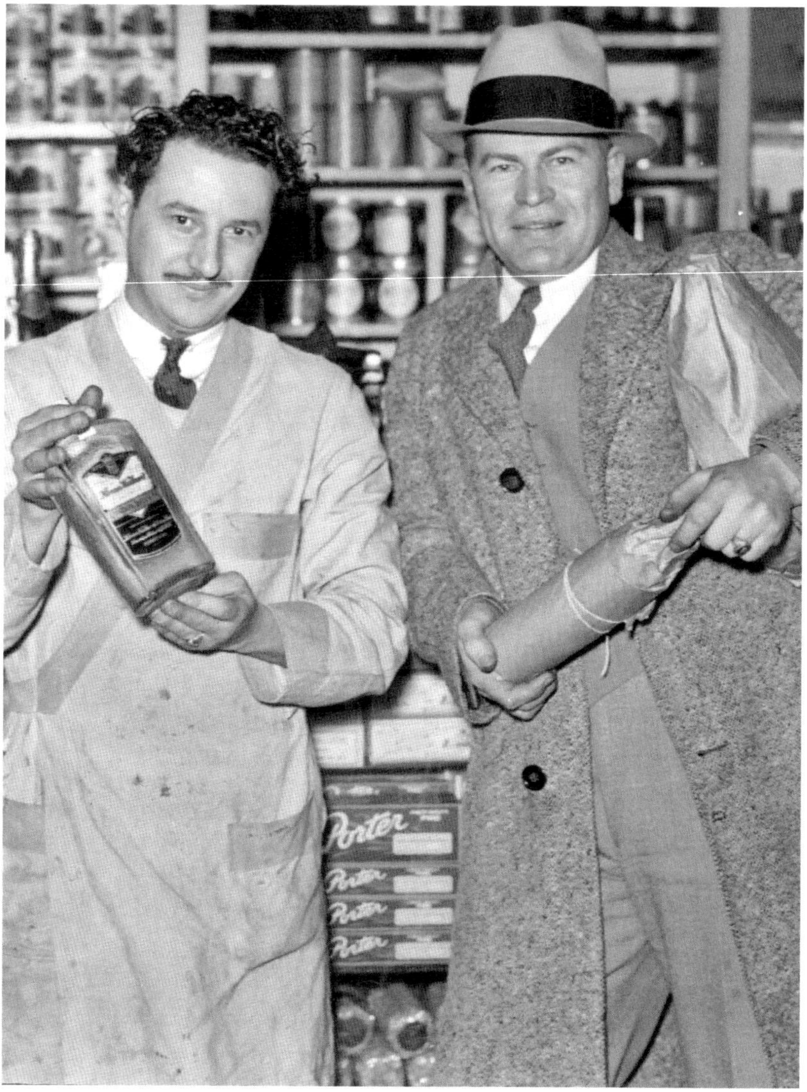


Intoxicating liquor became legal again in 1933. Strict regulation by the Oregon Liquor Control Commission and high taxes kept demand for contraband booze high, and bootlegging continued on a smaller scale for decades. *Oregon Historical Society.*

the 1890s, the Port of Portland worked closely with the U.S. Army Corps of Engineers to keep the channel open as it became a national priority.

In 1919, when James Polhemus became chief engineer of the Port of Portland, its governing body, the Port Commission, operated two dry docks and multiple freight terminals and owned its own dredging equipment. In 1921, the year Polhemus became general manager of the port, the commission was given responsibility for Swan Island and the development of the city's first airport. The Swan Island Airport opened in 1927 with a flying visit from Charles Lindbergh. Polhemus was a strong proponent of privately owned electric power, an issue that split the Republican Party in 1930. The issue came to a head as the federal government began making plans for large power-generating dams to be built on the Columbia River at Bonneville and Grand Coulee. Public power was not the only issue that caused dissension on the Port Commission. The other divisive issue was Polhemus's own management style.

Polhemus, a laissez-faire Republican, believed that his job as the manager of the publicly owned port was to facilitate business. Like most city officials at that time, he saw nothing wrong with using his public position for personal gain or to gain advantages for his friends. Many of the actions he took as port manager were considered to be unethical. For example, he sold off the port's dredging equipment, at sharply depreciated prices, to a company owned by his father-in-law, which promptly leased them back to the port at inflated prices; provided reduced prices at the dry dock to vessels from the States Steamship Line and other favored carriers; and selectively used dredging spoils to improve the value of property owned by favored people. By 1932, allegations of graft and corruption in port operations had become so common that the rules allowing the state legislature to appoint members to the Port Commission were changed; from now on, the members of the commission would be elected. Bert Haney, the federal prosecutor who sent Marie Equi to prison in 1920 and a public power advocate, was elected president of the commission. His first act was to call for a thorough investigation of the port's operations and its books.

Nationally, 1930 was a watershed year. The effects of the Great Depression were really being felt a year after the stock market crash. Faith in the capitalist system was shaken, and the economic theories of the Republican Party were discredited. The Democratic "New Deal" was sweeping Republicans out of office across the country. Oregon had been a "rock-ribbed" Republican state since Joe Simon took over the state senate in the 1880s. The Republicans in office didn't want to give up their power, but they had to get ahead of the Democrats somehow. Public power was the perfect issue. The popular idea was sweeping rural Oregon and Washington with public utility districts organized by communities large and small. George Joseph, a Portland attorney who favored public power, won the Republican nomination for governor in 1930 and looked like he would easily sweep the election, until he died of a heart attack.

With the Republican Party in disarray, the Central Committee bypassed public power primary candidates and turned to KKK-sympathizing Imperial Hotel mogul Phil Metschan Jr. for its candidate. The Progressive wing of the party was shocked, and prospects for the coming election looked dismal. Julius Meier, George Joseph's law partner, stepped forward as a public power candidate and, in an insurgent candidacy, swept the election, taking office in 1931. Acerbic Meier was a popular candidate and made a good foil for his more emotional opponent. As governor, he tried to run the state the way his good friend George Baker ran Portland. The major achievement of Meier's term was the founding of the Oregon State Police (OSP). Major General Smedley Butler, the heroic marine corps officer who would save the country from a military coup the following year, spent several weeks in Salem and Portland in his role as supervisor of the OSP during its formative days.

Meier was a popular and ruthless governor. Elected as a Progressive and reformer, Meier diligently went after corruption and graft everywhere his political enemies were practicing it. Phil Metschan Jr., a long-term member of the Port Commission who worked closely with Polhemus for years, was one of Meier's political enemies. Bert Haney's election was just the opportunity Meier was looking for, and he dispatched forensic accountant Frank Akin to look into the port's books. Akin's assignment was to "clean up" the port, but many believed he had been sent to do a "hatchet job" and to get both Polhemus and Metschan.

Akin was a large man who enjoyed the outdoor life and cultivated a "tough guy" image. An amateur gold and oil prospector, he was involved with several mining claims in eastern Oregon. After his death, rumors of Akin's "womanizing" were common. They may have been a "smoke screen," as his wife, Imo, insisted, or they may have been true. It is impossible to tell after more than eighty years. At the time of his death, Akin had just completed his investigation of the port and was scheduled to present his findings to the state legislature on the day after his murder. It had already been made public in Portland, though. Akin had found evidence of unethical behavior on the part of James Polhemus. Bert Haney called for the general manager's resignation. The timing of Akin's death was suspicious, and rumors that he had been killed because of his investigation were popular. Polhemus was eventually exonerated of the charges against him and went on to be general manager at Portland Electric Power Company.

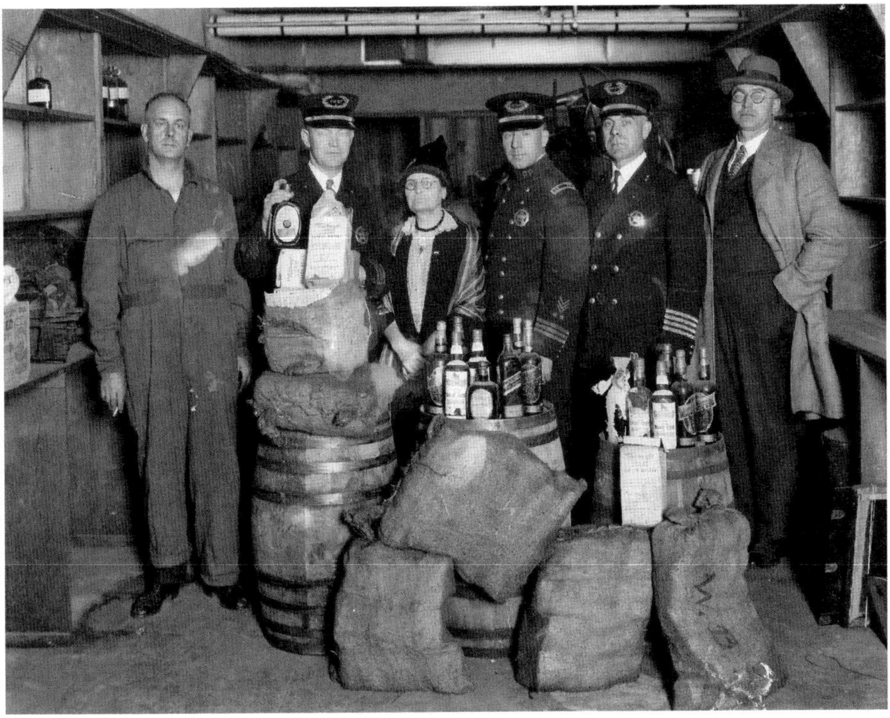

Leon Jenkins (second from right) was demoted to chief inspector in 1933 and took over command of the night watch. The new chief, Burton K. Lawson, a close friend of the new mayor, was considered an outsider by most members of the police bureau. Rival factions struggled for power within the bureau for the next few years. *Portland Police Historical Society.*

Akin's investigation of the Port of Portland was not the only potential motive for his murder. One month before his death, Akin had been named "special investigator" to look into allegations of financial misconduct in the city water bureau. Ever since Bull Run water began flowing through the faucets of Portland on January 2, 1895, our city drinking water has been considered to be among the best in the world. The water is good and has its own unique flavor, but the Portland Water Bureau has had an extremely controversial history. The construction of the system included "sweetheart deals"—in which favored vendors and contractors got city business at special rates—and allegations of corruption were not uncommon. By 1913, the bureau was running a deficit so large that historian Kimbark MacColl speculated about a giant leak somewhere. The "giant leak" was in the bureau itself, which sold much of its water without metering and provided free water to city departments and favored customers, such as Henry Pittock, who not only received free

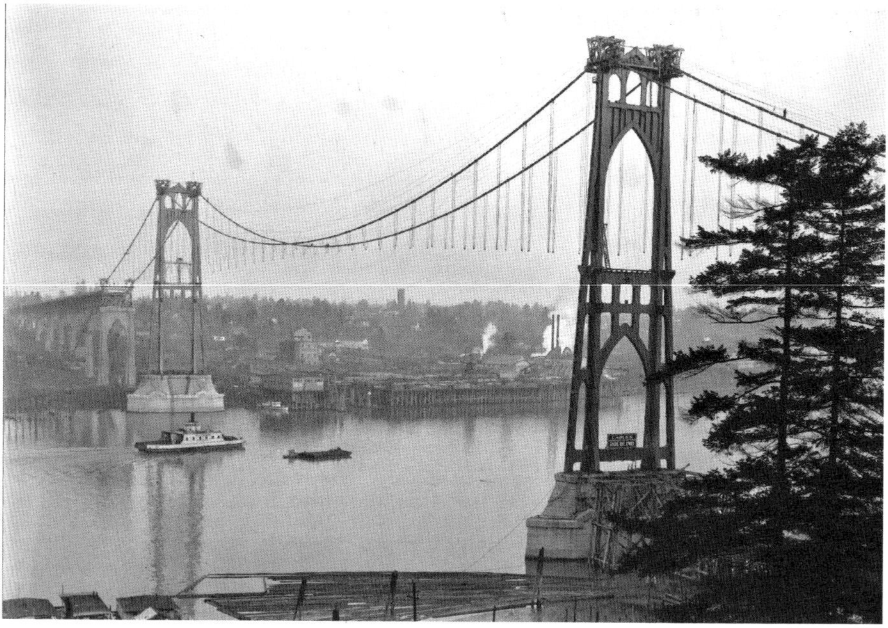

Public works projects were a favorite way to provide relief for unemployed Portlanders. Projects such as the St. Johns Bridge provided work for hundreds of hungry men and their families. *Portland City Archive.*

water but also had a special pipeline built to his hilltop mansion at the water bureau's expense.

Will Daly made his career by cleaning up the water bureau during his time on the Portland City Council. Between 1911 and 1917, Daly reformed operations and bookkeeping at the bureau, metered all water sales and ended free water deals for all except other city departments and oversaw the unionization of most of the city's employees outside the police bureau. His defeat at the polls in 1917 meant a return to business as usual at the water bureau under newly elected city commissioner John Mann. The 1920s were worse than business as usual, though. By the end of the decade, the water bureau was nearly $1 million in debt and corruption was rife. Councilman Mann's expensive Phaeton Sedan was paid for by the bureau, and he routinely assigned bureau employees to work for his personal projects, including construction jobs. In 1929, water bureau clerk Spear Herlinger was caught red-handed stealing $100 from the till. Auditors from the George Black Company estimated he had stolen nearly $20,000 over several years, but it was dangerous trying to find out. C.M. Lockwood, a Black Company accountant working late in the water bureau office at city hall on the evening of November 14, 1929, was narrowly missed by a three-pound rock hurled through the window behind him. He was cut by flying glass but not seriously injured. It was clear that someone didn't want anyone to look too closely at the water bureau's books. When John Mann was recalled from office and indicted in 1932, there was a public outcry to investigate the bureau. Frank Akin got the unpopular job and had just completed a preliminary report when he was murdered.

Even more fishy, Akin's report on the water bureau disappeared. After his death, police searching his apartment and his office were unable to locate Akin's report or any of his notes on the water bureau. His wife and friends said that the report would have been in his briefcase, which was found near the body; but it wasn't there. Seemingly, the only other copy of the report disappeared as well. City commissioner Jake Bennett, whom historian Jewel Lansing called the "most controversial councilmember to serve under George Baker" and who once came within a hair of being punched in the nose by His Honor, was the last one to see the report. Akin had given it to his associate Ray Lesher, who handed it over to Bennett and got a receipt for it. City auditor George Funk announced that Akin's report had found no evidence of wrongdoing and closed the investigation. Rumors swirled that there had been "hot stuff" in Akin's report, but when asked, Funk said he couldn't find it. Finally, he announced it had been given to Councilman Bennett and produced Lesher's receipt. After a year of fumbling the question, Bennett finally produced a receipt, showing that he had returned the report to the auditor's office. The *Oregonian*, under the clearly misleading headline "Missing Report Found," assured everyone that everything was all right.

The *Oregonian* quickly ruled out both the port investigation and the water bureau investigation as motives for Akin's murder, speculating that he was probably killed by someone burned in one of his mining deals or the jealous husband of one of his many lovers. His wife, Imo, insisted that Frank had been faithful to her. Her first words on hearing of her husband's death were, "Oh, Frank, why did you let them do it to you?" Whatever the reason, it was clear that Frank Akin had been killed on purpose, and it looked like a professional job.

There it stayed for almost three years—an enduring, stubborn mystery that fueled conspiracy theories of all kinds. Another crime only six months later began to shed light on how, if not why, Frank Akin's murder had been committed. On March 28, 1934, in the beach neighborhood of Erland's Point in Bremerton, Washington, two hundred miles north of Portland on the Olympic Peninsula, six people were massacred during a robbery in a

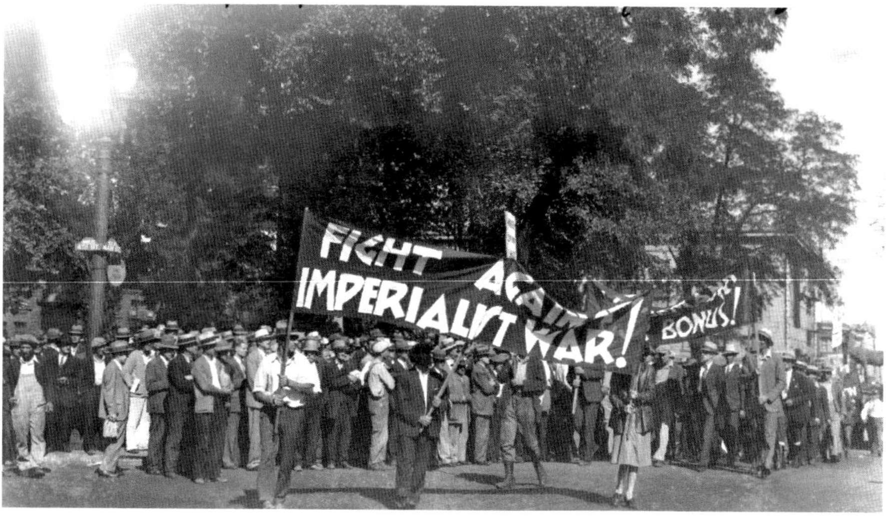


Economic hardship caused by the Great Depression made more and more people turn to the Communist Party for solutions. The emphasis of the police bureau became even more political than it had been, and it could spare few resources for catching criminals. *Portland City Archive.*

beach house. Frank Flieder, a retired Bremerton grocer; Anna Flieder, his wife; Eugene Chenevert, an ex-prizefighter and vaudeville entertainer; Margaret Chenevert, his wife and an actress; Magnus Jordan, a retired navy machinist and caretaker of the house; and Ezra "Fred" Bolcum, a Bremerton bartender, were all shot to death after they had been tied up and robbed. The Flieders were a well-liked, wealthy couple who were regular guests at the Wigwam in Olympia, Little Dutch Herman's joint.

The police investigation was a circus that included a Kitsap County sheriff's deputy who charged a crowd of 150 people twenty-five cents each to walk through the crime scene, scattering gum wrappers and litter as they went. One of the crowd members stole the stockings off of Anna Flieder's legs. The *Seattle Times* ran a contest for its readers to "Help Solve Bremerton's Murder Mystery!" offering one dollar for every story published and twenty dollars for the best story to "solve" the case. The winner was Martin Elliott, who submitted a "detailed confession" signed, "Sinisterly, The Killer." It was no wonder the police couldn't figure out who the killer was.

In September 1935, Larry Paulos and Joe Naples, two drug-addicted burglars from Seattle, were arrested in Yakima, Washington. Paulos and Naples were wanted in Seattle after a shootout with police and a high-speed chase out of town. The police knew the two men, though, and while waiting for the "gang" to show up at their Sumner, Washington hideout, they arrested Peggy Paulos, Larry's wife. Larry Paulos was a three-time loser facing "habitual criminal" charges on top of all the assault and robbery charges against him. He offered a deal to King County deputy O.K. Bodia; he would name the men who killed Frank Akin in return for a reduced sentence. The deal was made, and he named Jack Justice as the finger man who arranged the murder and Leo Hall as the triggerman. Paulos claimed that Justice had offered him $200 to beat Akin up, but he had been foiled when he confronted Akin with a gun at the door of his apartment and Akin fought back. Paulos was still bitter that Justice had refused to pay him the $200 for the unsuccessful attack.

Peggy Paulos, a waitress from Enumclaw, Washington, who had been questioned about her mysterious behavior in Bremerton on the night of the Erland's Point Massacre, must have been terribly frightened when she found out what her husband had revealed. She knew her life was forfeit, and she agreed to cooperate in return for protection. She told not only how Leo Hall shot Frank Akin in Portland but also how he had massacred six people at Erland's Point during a robbery because Anna Fleider's blindfold had slipped and she had seen Peggy's face. Hall decided not to leave any witnesses and killed all of the victims, even though three of them put up a terrible fight and almost overpowered him at one point. Leo Hall was a local tough who hung out at the Wigwam and was part of Walter Banaster's (aka Little Dutch Herman) gang. He had seen the wealthy couple gambling at the Wigwam and, thinking they were an easy mark for a robbery, followed them back to Bremerton. Peggy went along on a ride with "her boyfriend."

Akin's murder had been just another job for a "kill-crazy" gunman who worked for a local mobster. Jack Justice, a pimp, bootlegger and drug dealer from Portland, was an associate of Banaster's gang, sort of a middle manager doing his job, but there may have been a connection between the two men. Justice claimed to have met Akin in 1924 and invested in an oil well scheme in Wyoming that had come in a dry well. Justice claimed he lost $300 on the deal but didn't hold a grudge.

"Convict this man and you will open the door to those higher up," said Tom Handley, deputy district attorney, in his closing statement at Justice's 1936 trial. The jury agreed, but it really shut the door to those higher up. Justice was convicted of first-degree murder and sentenced to life, the best justice Frank Akin could get. Somehow Justice was out of jail when he died in 1951 in southeast Portland from heart attack behind the wheel of his car, just like Jim Elkins nearly twenty years later. Leo Hall went to the gallows in

Walla Walla. Peggy Paulos went into whatever witness protection there was in Washington in 1936. Larry Paulos went to jail for too short a time. No one ever found out who hired Jack Justice.

The Akin murder, despite the conviction and confession, has been considered unsolved ever since. The brutal shooting illustrated the lawlessness and fear that ruled the city. More than forty years later, when historian E. Kimbark MacColl wrote about the murder in *Growth of a City* (1979), his speculation centered on the port investigation, which was essentially completed by the time Akin died. He glossed over the water bureau situation, and in time, the case was forgotten or only vaguely remembered as an unsolved murder.

## CHAPTER 10

# THE HANGOVER

*Find the motive and in due course the criminal will be revealed.*
*—William Burns*

In April 1946, the Willamette was a contaminated, sickly river filled with toxins and bacteria. Extensive environmental studies conducted in 1934 discovered "an absolute barrier of denuded water about three miles long where oxygen loving forms of life cannot exist." It also found a "large amount of floating debris and sewage which is unsightly…the water has a very dirty brown color." Twelve years later, the population of the city had grown by more than 70 percent and the new shipbuilding industry, concentrated downriver from the city, had increased industrial pollution. Although its sights and scents were not always pleasant, the Willamette was still a favorite recreation site for Portlanders. That's how three people—H.C. Foster and James and Mary Rader—walking along the banks of the river on Friday, April 12, 1946, noticed the burlap bag swirling in the frothing eddies of the river near Milwaukie. Foster said he thought it was a "bag of drowned cats" as he pulled it to shore with a long stick. The three afternoon strollers were shocked when they opened the bag and found the torso of a woman, her head, arms and legs crudely severed.

It was the beginning of one of Portland's most enduring and unforgettable murder mysteries. Over the next few months, several more packages were found in the river, wrapped in newspaper and burlap and bound with identical twine and wire. Most of the woman's body parts were found, except

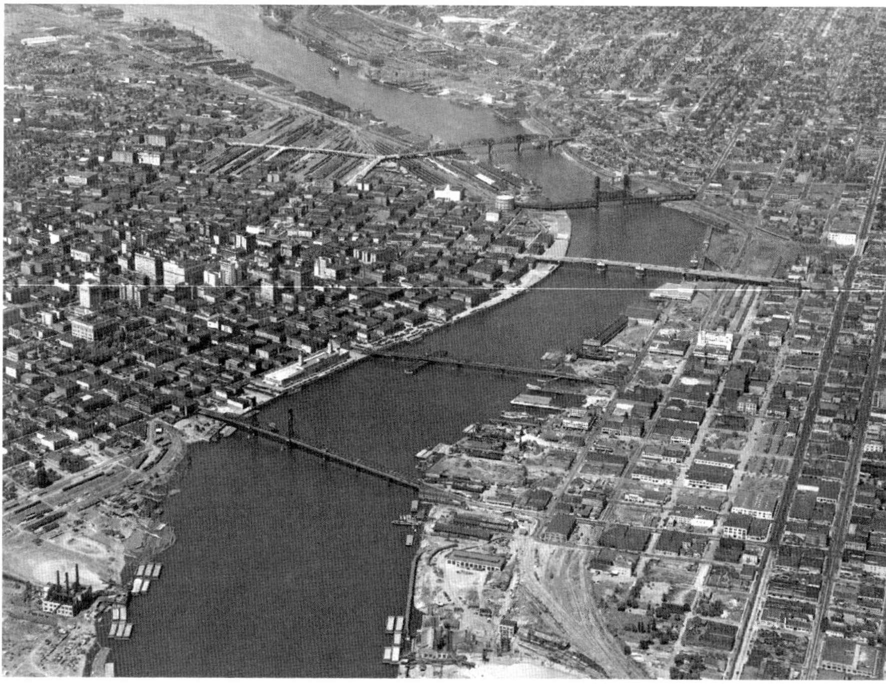

The Willamette River was a working river with severe pollution problems by the 1940s. It was not unusual to find bodies in the water, but it caused a sensation for a few months when the dismembered parts of a woman's body turned up in 1946. *Portland City Archive.*

the hands and feet, and despite having distinctive dentures and extensive dental work, the main way to identify corpses at the time, the woman's identity was never determined. The Oregon State Police and the Clackamas County Sheriff's Department conducted a thorough investigation, but they never looked too closely at the most likely source of the murder: organized crime in Portland.

The violent struggles for control that had dominated Portland's underworld in the 1930s had ended as Al Winter consolidated his power. Winter's alliance with Jim Elkins in the late '30s had guaranteed the muscle that Winter needed to exert control over his rivals, and one by one, Portland's violent criminals were carted off to jail, like Shy Frank Kodat in 1940, or took it on the lam, like Roy Moore in 1945. Jim Elkins and his boys kept things under control with the protection racket they ran against people who made their living from illegal businesses. Elkins had increased his own power, and the safety of his drug-smuggling operation, by cooperating with the coast guard and naval intelligence to ensure the "security" of Portland's waterfront during the Second World War. The election of Earl Riley, a protégé of George Baker, as mayor in 1940 ushered in a new era of organized vice and civic corruption in the Rose City. Riley and Al Winter, the son of Multnomah County judge John Winter, friends since childhood, and their relationship was even closer than that of Mayor Baker and Bobby Evans, although "Big Al" played a similar role to the one "Matchmaker Bobby" had played.

Old rivalries still split the police bureau, but under Chief Harry Niles, a lifelong officer with a long career in the police bureau, things had settled down considerably. Chief inspector Jenkins still controlled a large faction in the police bureau, and Captain Frank Ervin had expanded his own power in alliance with the ex-chief. Lieutenant James "Diamond Jim" Purcell, an ally of Jim Elkins who was involved in his own illegal businesses, was the rising star of the bureau. From chief of detectives he was promoted to captain and then to chief over the next six years. In 1946, Purcell was a newly appointed chief of detectives, overseeing major investigations. He and Captain James Fleming, who would also serve briefly as chief, had increased their own power and responsibility as Chief Niles's health failed. By 1946, when Niles was finally hospitalized and died shortly after, Purcell and Fleming were considered "co-chiefs." After Niles's hospitalization, Mayor Riley asked chief inspector Leon Jenkins to step back into the chief's office.

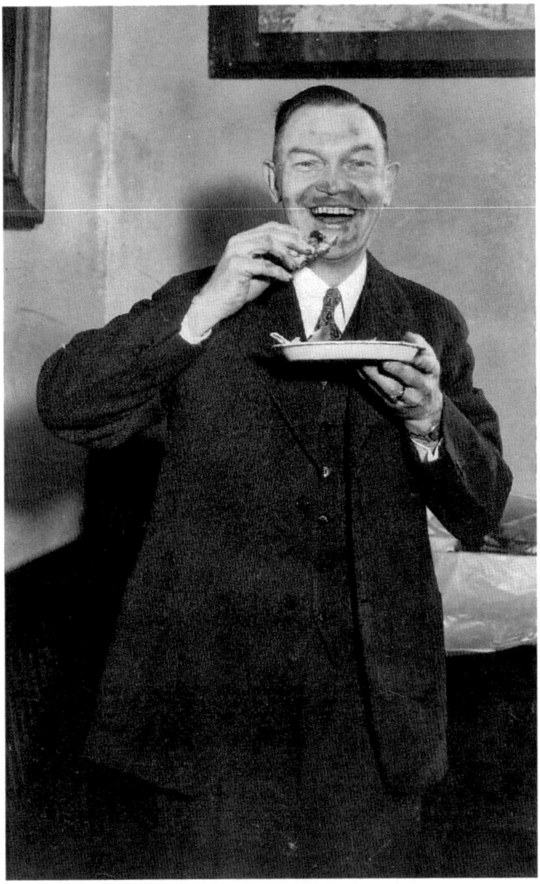

Leon Jenkins was chief inspector when this photo was taken, soon to be recalled as police chief. In this picture, he is celebrating his birthday with a specially made blackberry pie that weighed thirty pounds. *Portland Police Historical Society.*

The body parts in the river, which showed up steadily every four to six weeks throughout the summer and fall of 1946, caught the city's imagination, and the Torso Murder was on everyone's mind. Who was she? What had happened to her? Rumors that the woman had been tortured were steady, and the shocking nature of the crime and the grotesque method of disposing of her body titillated the public. The Clackamas County Sheriff, cooperating with the Oregon State Police, conducted a detailed investigation, leaving virtually no stone unturned. They ruled out dozens of women as the potential victim. They tracked down leads as far away as Indiana, Pennsylvania and Northern California, ruling out those that didn't pan out. Reading the investigative file of the many detectives and officers who doggedly tried to identify the woman in the river is a sad look into the lives of women in the 1940s and all the dangers, struggles and bad luck they faced.

Desperately sad letters begging for any information available about their mother, sister, daughter or wife who had gone missing and might be the torso victim fill the file, along with neatly typed reports of how the lead was investigated and the woman ruled out. Time and again, detectives documented neighbors' opinions that a man was a "mean drunk" or a relative's observation that he was "abusive to her." Sometimes the investigators would find a trail that looked like it might lead to the victim, like the case of Marie Diffin.

Marie Diffin was a part Native American woman, described as very beautiful, from Klamath Falls who seems to have led an extremely rough life. Growing up in a primitive mobile home in southern Oregon, she married early, to a man named George Diffin, a transient worker. Moving from place to place in rural Oregon, working mostly as an agricultural laborer or a domestic servant, Marie had several children with George. In the summer of 1944, Marie disappeared from the couple's home in Springfield, Oregon. George Diffin was described by numerous relatives and neighbors as "a mean drunk," "abusive" and "capable of anything." Claiming that he had heard rumors of Marie "chasing men" in Portland, Diffin didn't report Marie as missing until six years later, when his eighteen-year-old daughter insisted that he report her mother missing. Even Diffin's daughter said she wouldn't be surprised if her father had killed her mother and dumped her body into the river. Stories like the Diffin family's fill the case file.

Four years after the discovery of the body parts, Captain Vayne Gurdane of the Oregon State Police, who coordinated the joint investigation, must have felt they were on to a real lead. Although he was frugal, taking advantage of already planned travel and relying on cooperation from local police wherever he could, the OSP spent considerable resources to track the movements of Marie Diffin. George was quickly cleared as a suspect as police discovered that Marie had left Springfield with another man. Marie was never found. She was last seen in Klamath Falls, long after the torso showed up in the Willamette, promising to go "so far away no one will ever find us." She was obviously not the victim in the Torso Case, but the end of her story may not have been much happier.

The murder investigators did not completely ignore Portland's organized crime. In July 1951, at the request of Captain Gurdane, an unidentified FBI agent interviewed Roy Moore in his North Carolina prison cell. Moore talked openly about the murders that his gang committed, although he blamed all of the criminal activity on his partner, S.D. McLain (aka Doug Day), who had recently died in prison. Although Moore told a tantalizing but unconfirmable story about a woman who was dismembered and thrown into the Molalla River and gave surprising details on several murders that occurred in the early 1940s, he was not able to shed any light on the Torso Case. Sometimes Moore's testimony was unreliable, as he seemed to be holding a grudge against Day's lover and criminal partner, Jack Mann. In the interview report, Moore comes across as a braggart and liar. There is definitely some truth in what he says, but it is hard to tell how much is truth and how much is fiction.

Vayne Gurdane seems to have continued the investigation of the Torso Murder for more than a decade. It is very puzzling why Gurdane would say, as he was quoted in 1969, "The victim was never identified because the head was never found." Clearly, the head was found in October 1946, and Captain Gurdane knew it. The Clackamas County Sheriff's Department did a very thorough job of tracking down leads on dozens of women, but by the end of 1946, its investigation seems to have become very passive and by 1950 virtually nonexistent. It is as if the sheriff's department had given up on identifying the victim of the Torso Murder. Sometime in the 1950s, the physical evidence, which included the corpse's clothing, jaw bone and dentures, disappeared without a trace. There is no documentation on what happened to the evidence; current sheriff's department sources assume that the evidence was burned at some point, indicating that "at that time it was common for remains to be incinerated after a period of time had passed." Clackamas County reopened the homicide investigation in 2004, but there have been no new leads, and there is little hope of ever being able to solve the case with no living witnesses, no remains and no supporting documentation.

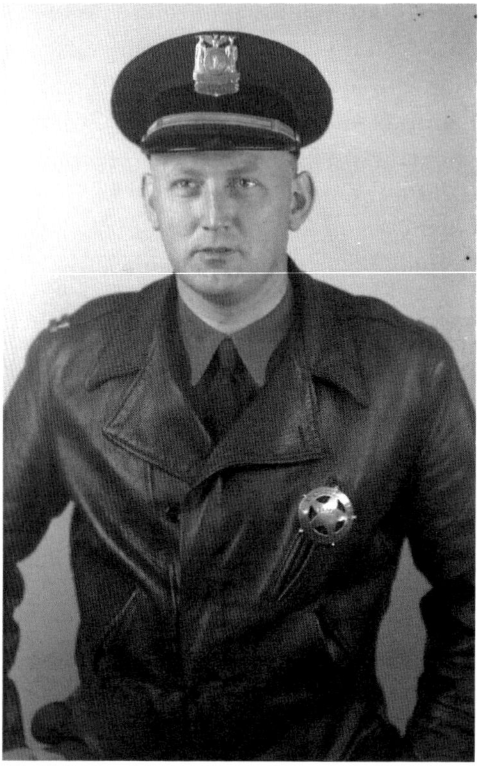

Jim Purcell was chief of detectives in 1946. He was very good at derailing investigations and covering up murders. Jim Elkins, local crime boss, paid Purcell well for his services. *Portland Police Historical Society.*

Why would such professional and dogged investigators just stop looking for answers? This is the key question of the Torso Case. As exemplified by Jim Purcell's investigation of the 1947 Tatum Murder and the 1948 Podlas/Schultze Case, described in detail in *Portland on the Take* (2014), the Portland Police Bureau had become very adept at containing murder investigations and influencing the sheriff's departments in their investigations of murder victims. One explanation for the end of the Clackamas County investigation would be that the PPB had asked them not to look any further. But why would they do that?

If someone involved in the police bureau had something to do with the case, or its cover up, Captain Purcell would have had no qualms about "containing" the investigation, and he would have had the necessary influence to derail a sheriff's department investigation, if not the state police investigation, which continued in other directions. But who could have been involved with the gruesome murder? Who would have the necessary motive?

Anna Schrader was never considered as the possible victim in the Torso Murder Case, but there are logical reasons that she should be. After the political struggle that followed the 1929 Schrader/Breuning scandal, Schrader had become surprisingly quiet. Withdrawing, or likely expelled, from the puritanical and exclusive Woman's Club, Schrader spent a quiet life in a southeast Portland home. Her husband, Edward Schrader, passed away in 1941, and there is little information on her past that point in time. The only clues as to her fate are three classified ads that appeared in the *Oregonian*. The first appeared on Anna Schrader's birthday, April 5, 1946. Designed to stay within the advertisement's ten-word limit, it said, "Anyone who knows the whereabouts of Ann [*sic*] Schrader please write N472 Oregonian." The same ad ran nine days later, two days after the discovery of the torso in the river; the third ran on April 19. The text of all three ads was the same. No trace of Anna Schrader has ever been found past that.

So, Anna Schrader disappeared in the spring of 1946, right before the body parts started showing up in the river. It is difficult to tell when the torso went into the river, but the best estimate was sometime in March. We don't know who placed the ad in the *Oregonian*, but if it was one of her friends, as it seems to have been, they wouldn't have waited too long. They would have waited at least a week or two, though, which could put her disappearance sometime in March. The age and physical description of the torso victim fits Schrader closely, right down to the size of the victim's brassiere. The clothing even seems to fit what we know of Schrader's taste, and the hairstyle of the corpse is consistent with hers. So there are the physical similarities and the coincidence of timing. But who would want Schrader dead?

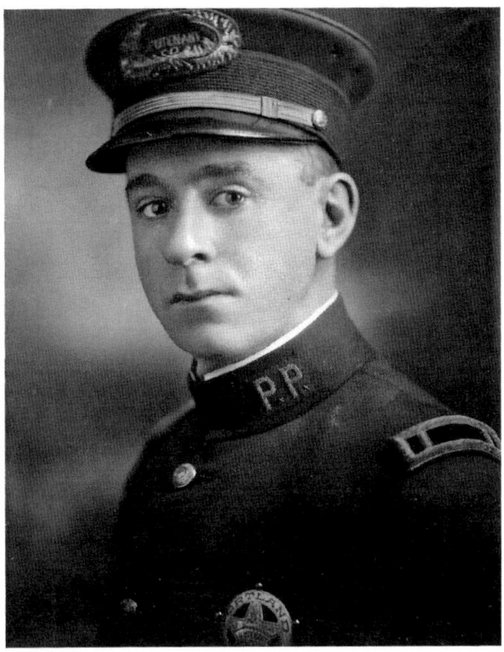

Frank Ervin was promoted to lieutenant in 1919 and became one of Chief Jenkins's most loyal supporters. Two memos he wrote to the chief in 1930 provide strong evidence that Jenkins had direct knowledge of illegal liquor distribution by police officers. *Portland Police Historical Society.*

It seems likely that Bill Breuning could have held a serious and long-standing grudge against his former lover. After his career was ruined by the 1929 scandal, Breuning had a very difficult time finding employment. He declared bankruptcy in 1930 and nearly lost his home that year. A few years later, he wrote a letter to a friend on the police force, begging him for a reference for a job at a local post office. In 1946, he was working as a "special officer," little more than a glorified security guard working the night shift and drawing his pay from the stores he guarded. It was a long way down for the dashing police lieutenant with a promising career he had enjoyed in 1921. He could easily have blamed Anna Schrader for the condition of his life and nursed a bitter grudge. The fact that the torso victim had been tortured with a blow torch on her "lower abdomen" seems like an extremely intimate type of violence that would be committed by a vengeful ex-lover. Whoever killed the torso victim hated her as much as Bill Breuning could have hated Anna Schrader.

With the physical evidence gone and all of the witnesses dead, we will never be able to tell for sure who the torso victim was. We will probably never be able to say with certainty what happened to Anna Schrader, either. The solution to the cases may rest on two vital questions: Why did Anna Schrader become silent after 1932? Why did she disappear in 1946? The two questions may be intertwined. Anna Schrader's past is very shadowy. Little is known about her first marriage, except that she was eighteen when she married before moving to Oregon in 1910. There is no evidence of how that marriage ended, either, or whether there were any children, which is likely considering her age at the time. Schrader had a history of adultery that may have carried over from her first marriage, and it is possible that there was an illegitimate child involved; Schrader's large extended family in the Midwest could easily have absorbed a child with no one ever knowing the truth. Any of those things could have been held over her head to ensure her silence, and the men who ran Portland had no qualms about using blackmail or even carrying out threats of violence to try and cover their crimes. Schrader was not the kind of person to be silenced by a bribe or payoff, but there was a large potential for blackmail, and fear could have kept her quiet for nearly fifteen years.

But why 1946? The answer to this goes back to the "bitter battle" that the police bureau waged against Schrader in the aftermath of the 1929 scandal. Besides the physical threats, shin-kicking attacks, bullets and bricks through the window and repeated car crashes that Schrader was subjected to, she was also harassed by a multitude of parking tickets. In 1930, a "fixed" parking ticket became the strongest piece of evidence, not only that Leon Jenkins knew about the liquor operation going on at Central Precinct, but also that he was being informed of details about the dirty fight being waged against Schrader. Two letters were found in the personnel file of Officer John Cordes, a friend of Schrader who fixed a ticket for her. The existing letters are carbon copies, and the originals are strangely not present in Jenkins's or Ervin's files. In the letters, requesting that the officer who fixed the ticket be disciplined, Captain Frank Ervin reminds the chief of the loyalty Ervin had shown in the "bitter battle" against Schrader and other enemies. During Schrader's time with the police bureau, she seems to have seen Jenkins as a father figure, an attitude he encouraged with his patriarchal management style. Schrader may have felt bitterly betrayed by his attitude and actions during the 1929 scandal, and much of her political activism was fueled by anger at Jenkins. It is not a stretch to think that in 1946 she felt sufficiently threatened by Jenkins's pending return to power as chief of police, and Anna Schrader was not a woman afraid to make threats. She may have finally decided to carry out the threat she had first made in 1929, to expose the inner machinations of the police bureau and "rock" Portland with her little black book containing her many secrets. We'll never know for sure, but historical speculation can be an interesting pastime.

# REFERENCES

The main sources of this work are the daily newspapers of Portland, especially the *Oregonian* and the *Portland Telegram*, as well as personnel and investigative files found in the Portland City Archive, Portland Police Museum and Clackamas County Sheriff's Department. The conclusions, opinions and speculation belong solely to the authors, but the following works informed that opinion.


Bingham, Edwin R. "Oregon's Romantic Rebels: John Reed and Charles Erskin Scott Wood." *Pacific Northwest Quarterly* 50, no. 3 (July 1959): 77–90.

Blalock, Barney. *Portland's Lost Waterfront: Tall Ships, Steam Mills and Sailors' Boardinghouses*. Charleston, SC: The History Press, 2012.

Boag, Peter. *Same Sex Affairs: Constructing and Controlling Homosexuality in the Pacific Northwest*. Berkeley: University of California Press, 2003.

———. "Sex & Politics in Progressive Era Portland & Eugene: The 1912 Same-Sex Vice Scandal." *Oregon Historical Quarterly* 100, no. 2 (Summer 1999): 158–81.

Brauer, Stephen. "Jay Gatsby and the Prohibition Gangster as Businessman." *The F. Scott Fitzgerald Review* 2 (2003): 51–71.

Caswell, John E. "The Prohibition Movement in Oregon: Part 1, 1836–1904." *Oregon Historical Quarterly* 39, no. 3 (September 1938): 235–61.

———. "The Prohibition Movement in Oregon: Part 2, 1904–1915." *Oregon Historical Quarterly* 40, no. 1 (March 1939): 64–82.

Chandler, JD. *Hidden History of Portland*. Charleston, SC: The History Press, 2013.

Chandler, JD, and JB Fisher. *Portland on the Take: Mid-century Crime Bosses, Civic Corruption and Forgotten Murder*. Charleston, SC: The History Press, 2014.

Daley, Shawn. "Will Daly 1869–1924." Oregon Encyclopedia. http://www.oregonencyclopedia.org/articles/daly_will_1869_1924_/#.VhwRB_lViko.

Dever, Lem A. *Masks Off! Confession of an Imperial Klansman*. Vancouver, WA: Privately Published, 1925.

Dupay, Don. *Behind the Badge in River City: A Portland Police Memoir*. Portland: Oregon Greystone Press, 2015.

Goff, Brian, and Gary Anderson. "The Political Economy of Prohibition in the United States, 1919–1933." *Social Science Quarterly* 75, no. 2 (June 1994): 270–83.

Guthrie, John J., Jr. "Hard Times, Hard Liquor and Hard Luck: Selective Enforcement of Prohibition in North Florida, 1928–1933." *Florida Historical Quarterly* 72, no. 4 (April 1994): 435–52.

Hales, Barbara. "Woman as Sexual Criminal: Weimar Construction of the Criminal Femme Fatale." *Women in German Yearbook* 12 (1996): 101–21.

Harland, Marion. "Truth About Female Criminals." *North American Review* 150, no. 398 (January 1890): 138–40.

Hibschman, Harry. "Prohibition's Absurdities." *North American Review* 230, no. 1 (July 1930): 36–43.

Hodges, Adam J. "Enemy Aliens and Silk Stocking Girls: The Class Politics of Internment in the Drive for Urban Order During World War I." *Journal of the Gilded Age and Progressive Era* 6, no. 4 (October 2007): 431–58.

———. "Oregon Voices: At War Over the Espionage Act in Portland." *Oregon Historical Quarterly* 108, no. 3 (Fall 2007): 474–86.

Jackson, Kenneth T. *The Ku Klux Klan in the City, 1915–1930*. Chicago: I.R. Dee, 1992.

Jaros, David Michael. "Perfecting Criminal Markets." *Columbia Law Review* 112, no. 8 (December 2012): 1947–91.

Jensen, Kimberly. "Neither Head nor Tail to the Campaign: Esther Pohl Lovejoy and the Oregon Woman Suffrage Victory of 1912." *Oregon Historical Quarterly* 108, no. 3 (Fall 2007): 350–83.

Johnson, Mueller J. "Updating the Accounts: Global Mortality of the 1918–1920 'Spanish' Influenza Pandemic." *Bulletin of Historic Medicine* 76 (2002): 105–15.

Johnston, Robert. *The Radical Middle Class: Populist Democracy and the Question of Capitalism in Progressive Era Portland, Oregon*. Princeton, NJ: Princeton University Press, 2003.

Kyvig, David E. "Women Against Prohibition." *American Quarterly* 28, no. 4 (Autumn 1976): 465–82.

Lansing, Jewel. *Portland: People, Politics and Power, 1851–2001*. Corvallis: Oregon State University Press, 2003.

Lansing, Jewel, and Fred Leeson. *Multnomah: The Tumultuous Story of Oregon's Most Populous County*. Corvallis: Oregon State University Press, 2012.

Largent, Mark A. "The Greatest Curse of the Race: Eugenic Sterilization in Oregon, 1909–1983." *Oregon Historical Quarterly* 103, no. 2 (Summer 2002): 188–209.

MacColl, E. Kimbark. *Growth of a City: Power and Politics in Portland, Oregon, 1915 to 1950*. Portland, OR: Georgian Press, 1979.

———. *Shaping of a City: Business and Politics in Portland, Oregon, 1885–1915*. Portland, OR: Georgian Press, 1976.

Mangun, Kimberly. *A Force for Change: Beatrice Morrow Cannady and the Struggle for Civil Rights in Oregon, 1912–1936*. Corvallis: Oregon State University Press, 2010.

Marsh, Floyd. *20 Years a Soldier of Fortune*. Portland, OR: Binford & Mort, 1976.

Munk, Michael. *Portland Red Guide—Second Edition*. Portland, OR: Ooligan Press, 2002.

Murphy, Mary. "Mothers and Drinking Daughters: Gender and Prohibition in Butte, MT." *American Quarterly* 46, no. 2 (June 1994): 174–94.

Myers, Gloria E. *A Municipal Mother: Portland's Lola Greene Baldwin, America's First Police Woman*. Corvallis: Oregon State University Press, 1995.

Oakley, Imogen B. "The Prohibition Law and the Political Machine" in "Prohibition and Its Enforcement," special issue, *Annals of the American Academy of Political and Social Science* 109 (September 1923): 165–74.

Pauly, Thomas H. "The Criminal as Culture." *American Literature History* 9, no. 4 (Winter 1997): 776–85.

Pegram, Thomas R. "The Anti-Saloon League and the Ku Klux Klan in 1920s Prohibition Enforcement." *Journal of the Gilded Age and Progressive Era* 7, no. 1 (January 2008): 89–119.

Portland, Oregon. "Influenza Encyclopedia." University of Michigan Library. http://www.influenzaarchive.org/cities/city-portland.html.

Rose, Kenneth D. "The Labbe Affair and Prohibition Enforcement in Portland." *Pacific Northwest Quarterly* 77, no. 2 (April 1986): 42–51.

Sanchez, Tanya Marie. "The Feminine Side of Bootlegging." *Louisiana History* 41, no. 4 (Autumn 2000): 403–33.

Schaller, Michael. "The Federal Prohibition of Marijuana." *Journal of Social History* 4, no. 1 (Autumn 1970): 61–74.

Soden, Dale E. "The Woman's Christian Temperance Union in the Pacific Northwest: The Battle for Cultural Control." *Pacific Northwest Quarterly* 94, no. 4 (Fall 2003): 197–207.

Stewart, Ella Seass. "Woman Suffrage and the Liquor Traffic" in "Women in Public Life" special issue, *Annals of the American Academy of Political and Social Science* 56 (November 1914): 143–52.

Tobie, Harvey Elmer. "Oregon Labor Disputes, 1912–1923: The Living Wage." *Oregon Historical Quarterly* 48, no. 1 (March 1947): 7–24.

Toy, Eckard V., Jr. "Oregon at War." *Oregon Historical Quarterly* 102, no. 4 (Winter 2001): 414–33.

Washington, Booker T. "Negro Crime and Strong Drink." *Journal of the American Institute of Criminal Law and Criminology* 3, no. 3 (September 1912): 384–92.

Wiegand, Wayne A. "Oregon's Public Libraries During the First World War." *Oregon Historical Quarterly* 90, no. 1 (Spring 1989): 39–63.

Woolley, Ivan M. "The 1918 'Spanish Influenza' Pandemic in Oregon." *Oregon Historical Quarterly* 64, no. 3 (September 1963): 246–58.

Young, F.G. "Oregon History for the Oregon System." *Quarterly of the Oregon Historical Society* 12, no. 3 (September 1911): 264–68.

# INDEX

## J



## K



## L



## M



## N



## O



## P

## Y

# ABOUT THE AUTHORS

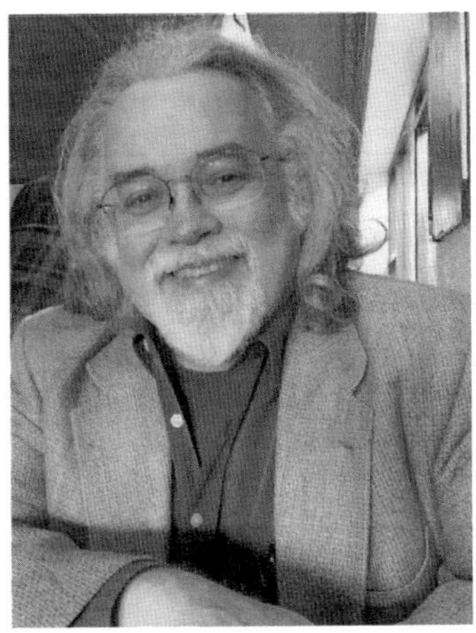

JD Chandler, a former labor union activist, is a native Oregonian. He is the author of three previous books on Portland history: *Hidden History of Portland, Oregon* (2013), *Murder and Mayhem in Portland, Oregon* (2013) and *Portland on the Take: Mid-Century Crime Bosses, Civic Corruption & Forgotten Murders* (2014). In addition, he is the author of two blogs ("Weird Portland" and "Slabtown Chronicle") and a popular podcast (*Murder by Experts*) concerning Portland history. You can keep track of his creative efforts on his webpage www.patreon.com/jdchandler.

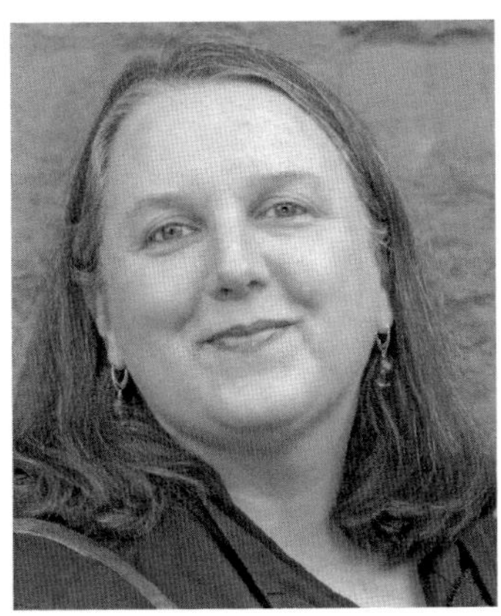

Theresa Griffin Kennedy is a writer, poet, social activist and painter of abstract mixed-media art. In 2013, she completed a master's degree at Portland State University in adult education, leadership and policy, with a master's certificate in teaching adult learners. Her goal, when time allows in 2016, is to teach incarcerated offenders and community college students creative writing with a focus on the human relationship to past trauma and the mechanisms of survival. Kennedy has written articles and essays on the rights of those living in the Middle East, as well as on issues pertaining to the homeless, the mentally ill, rape, sustainable building renovation, censorship, nonviolent protest and even the Iranian Blogosphere. She is the author of two books, including a volume of poetry, *Blue Reverie in Smoke*, published by Oregon Greystone Press. She lives in Portland, Oregon, and is married to Don DuPay, a retired police detective and longtime writer.

*Visit us at*
www.historypress.net

*This title is also available as an e-book*